*For Sarah* [handwritten]

**BITE-SIZED** book

# Hawk and Hyena

*When snapped (me, not at me!)* [handwritten]

## What Really Happened to The Serpent

## Farrukh Dhondy

*Best,* [handwritten]

*[signature]* [handwritten]

Cover by
**Dean Stockton**

Published by Bite-Sized Books Ltd 2021
©Farrukh Dhondy 2021

Bite-Sized Books Ltd 8th Floor, 20 St. Andrews Street, London EC4A 3AY, UK

**Registered in the UK. Company Registration**

**No: 9395379**

**ISBN: 9798760300867**

*"I kill where I please because it is all mine.*
*There is no sophistry in my body:*
*My manners are tearing off heads –*
*The allotment of death…….."*

HAWK ROOSTING

by Ted Hughes

*"I am waiting*
*for the foot to slide,*
*for the heart to seize,*
*for the leaping sinews to go slack . ."*

HYENA

by Edwin Morgan

# Preface

Before Charles Sobhraj called me in 1997, at my office at Channel 4 TV, where I worked as a Commissioning Editor, I had read one book about him. That was Richard Neville and Julie Clarke's novelistic reconstruction from their interviews with Sobhraj in Delhi's Tihar jail in 1977, soon after his initial arrest in India. It was entitled Shadow of the Cobra and subtitled The Life and Crimes of Charles Sobhraj.

After that phone call and a few subsequent meetings with Sobhraj, I got hold of another account of this life and these crimes. This, Serpentine by Thomas Thompson, was called by the author "A true Odyssey of love and evil". He claims in a preface that it is "in essence a true story." He admits to changing some of the names, which Neville and Clarke don't bother to do, as they claim that they have constructed their book from Sobhraj's first-hand account.

A casual reading of this second book didn't compel me at the time to make comparisons between the accounts. Neither of the books deals with Sobhraj's fate or follies during his stay in Tihar or after his release in 1997. Although he was immediately rearrested by the Indian police on further charges and held for a few days, fortuitous circumstances, which I recall in this memoir, followed by diplomatic deals, had him released and deported to France.

On his release, and as he was being deported to France, Richard Neville was commissioned to interview him again, this time on CNN for international distribution. In this interview, Charles denied ever having confessed to the murders that Neville and Clarke, twenty years earlier, had described in gruesome detail in their book. It was their claim, however, that these were accurate representations of what Charles had told them while beginning his sentence in Tihar.

In 1988, eight years before this abject denial, while Sobhraj was still in jail in India, Neville and Clarke's book was turned into an Australian-produced and universally broadcast TV serial, starring Art Malik in the central role. Shadow of the Cobra features, in heroic detail, the role of the Dutch diplomat Herman Knippenberg whose efforts led to Sobhraj's arrest in Thailand in the mid-seventies.

In 2021, the BBC released a series called The Serpent which diligently traces Sobhraj's life and crimes through Knippenberg's efforts at tracking them down and securing the arrest of Charles, his Canadian girlfriend Marie-Andre and his Indian accomplice Ajay Chowdhury for several murders in Thailand.

Both these serials end with Sobhraj's arrest in Thailand. That was not where he was jailed. Pending his conviction and sentencing for eleven murders in Thailand, Charles and his accomplices escaped, probably by bribing their Thai prison guards, and continued their trail of criminal activity in India where both Charles and Marie-Andre were arrested, tried, convicted and jailed. It was in this Indian jail that Neville and Clarke interviewed Sobhraj.

A third effort at screening his adventures, concentrating on a fabricated account of his escape from Tihar jail and his recapture and return to it with an enhanced sentence, was the Bollywood film 'Charles and Me'.

The talented actor Randeep Hooda, who played Sobhraj in this Bollywood production, was made-up to strikingly resemble Sobhraj. He happens to be a friend. At a party in Mumbai at my niece's house, while the film was being processed and publicised, he confided that the film follows the story that appeared in the Indian press, the one that Sobhraj had sold them.

It was a contrivance and fantasy with a purpose. Sobhraj had already told me the truth about this escape. And yet the film had recreated this fantasy, falling for the plot about sweets at a birthday celebration laced with soporific drugs that Charles had used as a cover for his escape. When Charles told me the truth about this escape he seemed extremely proud that he had perpetrated the fantasy which the film now portrayed.

I asked Randeep if he believed the film's plot and premise and when he said he did, I asked him what presents he had asked Santa Claus to bring him for Christmas. He wasn't amused.

In 1997, where this memoir begins, I was astounded to get a call from Charles. Over the next years I made his acquaintance, that of his ex-wife Chantal and that of his Chinese girlfriend whom he called Roseanne, though that isn't her real name. As a writer of books, films and TV and being a commissioner of TV programmes at the time, I indulged and enthusiastically encouraged the acquaintance with the prospect of collecting material for one or other form of documentary or fiction about the life, crimes, evolution, motives of a known and perhaps self-confessed serial killer.

Aware of his horrific crimes, I remained wary and kept the relationship at the level of acquaintance. I never invited him home in London and we always met in public places, in London and in Paris. Chantal, who had returned after more than twenty years to be with him, abandoning her two daughters and American husband, spoke to me about his life and what she knew about his crimes.

Little did I think or realise when he first called me, that Charles Sobhraj would attempt to involve me in his life of

3

international dodgy deals, communications of a clandestine sort with the CIA, offers of assistance and betrayal to governments and sordid recollections from his past. Perhaps I was ready and even eager, as I've said, for the last --- but unaware that any of the rest would come my way.

In 2003 Charles was arrested in Kathmandu and convicted of a murder he had allegedly committed twenty-two years previously. The BBC serial The Serpent ends with a note which says no-one knows why he went to Kathmandu and risked arrest.

I do.

In 2008 I published a fictionalised account of the Charles Sobhraj story, drawing on my own acquaintance with Charles, Roseanne and Chantal. The novel, The Bikini Murders, featured a fictional character called Johnson Thaat, but the Indian media pounced upon it and determinedly identified him as Charles Sobhraj.

Being in Mumbai when the book was launched, I was invited onto a TV programme by the notoriously pugnacious presenter Arnab Goswami. I readily accepted the invitation – one writes to be read.

Goswami went through the motions of asking me about the provenance of the book and then said he had a little surprise for me. The programme cut to Kathmandu jail, where the programme had sent their crew. Sobhraj appeared and virtually said he identified with the character in the book and that he would sue the publishers and myself for untold sums. He said "Farrukh is a 'middle-man'" by which I assumed he meant a pimp.

"If Nelson Mandela had called me that, I'd be deeply offended, but you can say what the fuck you like," I said.

Arnab had a second trick up his televisual sleeve. The programme cut to Paris, to a person who identified herself as Charles's lawyer and again announced that she was going to win millions of Euros or Pounds, or whatever, in libel damages from me.

Apart from the fact that I didn't have any assets, besides those that would buy me an entrance ticket to the Louvre, my own lawyer friends and Harper Collins' lawyers said a fellow serving life for murder couldn't have his reputation ruined by my book. Besides, was this lady lawyer saying that Charles identified with the murders my character had committed?

When this lawyer came on the screen, I recognised her from her name and from photographs in the media.

"This is the lady married to the killer known as The Jackal who is in jail for life in France. She has represented illustrious fellows such as Milosevich and Saddam Hussein and now Charles. So, see you in court," I said.

They didn't sue.

During the long pre-production period of the BBC drama and the pre-publicity it received, several investigative journalists from newspapers, magazines and TV approached me with requests for an exchange of information. They may have seen several articles I had written or perhaps read The Bikini Murders. One of them, Andrew Anthony, said he had come to me on the recommendation of Charles to whom he had spoken in Kathmandu jail.

In this memoir I have recalled the facts of my encounters with Sobhraj and attempted to piece together accounts of the events I did not and could not have witnessed, but were in one form or another, related to me. Some of these accounts are by definition second-hand and hearsay. For instance, Chantal told me things which she hadn't witnessed but had perhaps heard from Charles himself.

\*

If the readers of this memoir can be bothered with comparisons, they will probably discover that very many of the 'facts' in both the books, that of Neville and Clarke and that of Thompson, and some of the speculations and reconstructions in the film, and at least one of the serials, are fanciful, misguided or possibly wrong. I have to say 'possibly' as it may be that the accounts I have gleaned from Charles himself, Chantal and the investigative reporters on the trail of the story may also be constructions in the annals of this prophet of deceit.

\*

That first book in which he features, purports to be based on Charles's confessions but reads at times like an account of detection on the part of the writers. Reading the book and speaking to him later, I was aware that Sobhraj was careful to not offer these confessions on a tape recorder and give Neville evidence which could convict him in a court of law.

By the time Neville interviewed him, Sobhraj had established himself in Tihar jail, initially by smuggling diamonds into the prison by swallowing them in metal capsules and retrieving them from his shit. He traded them in exchange for a few comforts and gained power over the warders he had bribed, threatening them with exposure because he had witnesses to their corruption. He inveigled more and more warders and in a few months' time he had a comfortable bed and soft mattress, a refrigerator, a mobile phone, a computer, a desk and food brought in from restaurants of his choice outside. He began to assume his princely status and treated the warders as his retainers.

Neville and Clarke interviewed him not as wretched prisoner, but as the Prince of Tihar.

The second book by Thomas Thomson sold well but Charles told me he got nothing out of it as Thomas wrote it without reference to him. He didn't like that. And now that he was out, there was nothing he could do to Thomson. Thomson was dead. Natural causes.

I have made no investigative efforts myself. What follows is a recollection of my acquaintance and dealings with Charles and Chantal and an attempt at reconstructing the life and crimes of this person who killed and preyed on the dead from the recollection of events as Charles or Chantal related them to me. They may, now and then, be peppered with accounts that journalists in our conversations have assured me are unquestionable facts.

Hawks attack and kill the weaker species – hyenas prey on the still dead.

# 1

Ajay Chowdhury, an Indian in his twenties, a drop-out from Delhi university who has abandoned his family and gone trekking on the hippy trail, and Charles Sobhraj, half Indian-Sindhi and half Vietnamese, who has assumed the identity of Alain Gautier, drive down from Bangkok to the Thai coast outside Pattaya. In the back of the car is Teresa Knowlton, a young American tripping, in both senses, in Bangkok.

She is drugged and drowsy. According to Charles, she has drugged herself. It's twilight and Charles recalls that they were to lodge in a holiday hut in Pattaya. He said Teresa had very clearly signalled to him, when they partied in Bangkok, that she wanted him to fuck her. They had to get away from his girlfriend Marie-Andre who lived with Charles in a flat in Kanit House, a complex of rented apartments with a swimming pool for tenants and guests.

Charles had managed this dodge, leaving Marie-Andre behind. Ajay, his new 'assistant' had insisted on coming for the ride and, Charles said, had noticed that Teresa was carrying a small fortune in dollars and travellers' cheques, something he knew nothing about.

As they drove down along the coast, they decided to park the car and go for a swim. Teresa had prepared herself, wearing a flowered bikini under her loose clothes and was looking forward to a dip in the tropical waters, perhaps under the eye of a romantic moon. Charles recalls that they entered the water, with Teresa reviving from her grogginess in the warm waters. Ajay was looking solemn as he swam after Teresa who had gone out into the deep water.

Before Charles realised what was going on and while he couldn't quite make out what was happening a little distance away as he was still knee deep in the water, he heard Teresa's short, sharp shout. It wasn't a scream. Charles waded and swam out to where the two of them were. Ajay's head was above the waters, but his arms were holding Teresa down under them. Before Charles could stop him, Ajay had drowned the poor bikini-clad girl.

They had no option but to leave her in the water and get away, which is what they did.

According to the accounts in the books, though Thompson changes her identity, Teresa's body was found the next day by a fisherman or by a cyclist who noticed the body on the beach and thought it was one of the hippy tourists. On his way back to his village, the same cyclist is supposed to have approached the body and found Teresa dead.

There is no evidence that Ajay took the initiative to murder any of their victims but he undoubtedly followed Charles like a loyal lap-dog and participated in the murders that followed, poisoning drinks, injecting victims with poisons he had been taught the dosage of and setting fire to dead bodies after pouring petrol on them. He was, by all accounts, a willing if not enthusiastic tool. Teresa was murdered, as the autopsy proved, through drowning, but she was already sedated with a dose so heavy that it could have been intended as fatal.

Ajay had, a few days previous to this murder, been recruited by Charles and hadn't till then been tested by Charles for his dependability. It is speculative, but likely, that Charles wanted to test this future accomplice in murder by enticing him into being active in the drugging and drowning of Teresa. So, contrary to Charles's version of Ajay wanting a holiday weekend in Pattaya, he may have insisted on his coming with him when they took

Teresa to a club and drugged her. Charles may have planned to throw her body into the sea, even hoping that any post mortem would conclude she had drugged herself and gone for a swim and drowned. But with Ajay complicit in the act, he would have a hold on him which would compel him to join the murder spree which followed.

Did Ajay protest as they carried the comatose body to the waves, saying that this girl was still alive and what the hell was Charles making him do? And did Charles push the now awake Teresa's head under water to drown her or did he get Ajay through complicity or blackmail to do it? By all accounts Ajay willingly participated in all the evil that followed. And then paid for it?

By the time I heard Charles' version of Teresa's murder, Ajay had been missing for over twenty years and has never been accounted for. By all accounts, he accompanied Charles to Malaya, to where they escaped from Thailand, perhaps travelling under an assumed name of someone he'd murdered. There are no accounts of Ajay being seen after that in India or Bangkok or anywhere else. Charles went on to India with Marie-Andre -- Ajay didn't.

I asked Charles what happened to Ajay in front of Chantal. Charles said he didn't know, and shrugged but I noticed Chantal briefly smiling. Did she know how Ajay had been disposed of?

It's not difficult to speculate on a motive for this disappearance. He knew too much and may have begun to make demands with implied threats of blackmail. He may even have threatened to leave the close, murderous partnership – something that Charles could not risk. That Charles would know how to kill and dispose of even his closest partner in crime is in no doubt. No body has ever been found and if the Malaysian police found and

10

registered a body, perhaps charred beyond recognition, they didn't identify it as that of Ajay Chowdhury.

"I don't know, he disappeared!"

Charles has trained himself to give away no information or inkling of his mental processes through his features. One more murder would have, in Sobhraj's book, been deemed necessary.

# 2

"My name is Charles Sobhraj, you might have heard of me," said the voice on the phone.

My secretary had passed on the call, saying this person had called ten times and she had warded him off, but he was dogged about wanting to speak to me and wouldn't tell her what it was about. He had finally told her it was personal and urgent, so she thought she'd better put him through.

I took the call. There was Charles Sobhraj identifying himself on the phone.

"You're the serial killer," I said, hesitating before using the phrase. Should I be diplomatic, use a euphemism. The hell with it, I thought in that instant, I'll see if he acknowledges such a description. The game was on.

He drew breath the other end and picked up the glove.

"You could put it that way," he said.

So many encounters later, I would learn that he not only acknowledged the description, while never admitting or confessing to killing anyone, he was proud of it. He would say, "People, even criminals, respect me for being a super criminal."

On that first phone call I was naturally curious as to why this notorious character was calling.

"Are you speaking from jail?" I asked.

"No, no that is all over. I am in Paris and completely free. But I need your help. You see, like you I am a writer. Now listen: You were with my cousin Ram Advani in college in

Poona and then you were both writing for the Poona Herald – you remember?"

His accent was a caricatured French with the 'i's becoming 'ee' and the emphases on syllables going haywire. "... and my cousin said you were the best man in Europe to help me."

"How can I help you?" I asked, curious and feeling lucky. It was as though a subject for a sure-fire TV programme had walked through the door. He had killed people in Thailand, India and Nepal, maybe in Pakistan, Iran, Greece and Turkey in the 1970s. Audience memories are short. But a confession would jog them. Did he want to confess?

Some part of any Commissioning Editor's job at Channel 4 was to grab the imagination of audiences. Increasingly the TV world was inclined, if not anxious, to find that which would bring in the audience and could be seen as culturally or educationally innovative. My colleagues had been grasping for something to make the millions switch on.

One female colleague said she'd found a scientist who could measure sexual arousal and satisfaction through the chemical and electrical impulses of brain and body and could calibrate them precisely. She proposed a series to explore whether big pricks really made for greater satisfaction, and whether thinking about a woman other than their wives turned men on. "The greatest leap forward in sexual awareness since feminism," is how she put it. "Lots of explicit stuff, scientifically cloaked of course." The series never got made. Another colleague suggested family games in which they took away prizes for the wrong answers or choices. A truck would wait outside your house and be filmed carting away your telly, fridge, video camcorder, beds, sofas and all. That never got made either. But I had the ace around the table. Or would have had.

As I spoke to CS that first time, my mind turned to the bouquet I would have to construct with this Venus' fly-trap at the centre. 'An exploration of the existential man--—a mind without morality --- the banality of evil....' The banality of all propaganda and euphemism.

"I want you to help me get my book published. I am writing a book."

"What book is this?"

"My memoirs in jail. I spent twenty years in Tihar Jail in Delhi, you know."

"Yes, I know. I've followed your career."

"Everybody has." There was a swell of pride in the voice and then the qualification of a pretended modesty. "But these newspapers don't all tell the truth eh, Mr Dhondy? You know that. They make up stories. But I can tell the true story eh?"

"All of it?" I asked.

"We shall discuss that. But I have a manuscript. Maybe you can read it. My cousin tells me I can trust you completely."

"I remember him.," I said. "We used to work as cub reporters on the Poona Herald all those years ago when we were in college."

"I can come and see you? I can come today or tomorrow to London. I need to clear up some travelling restriction with the French police, you know."

" I understand," I said. "But tell me when you can make it."

14

"Give me your home address and phone number," he said.

"Oh.. I work very hard, just call me at the office and I'll give you my mobile," I said. "Home is quite some distance from the centre and I work all hours so we can meet at the office."

"That is good," he said. He was perhaps used to people not divulging their home addresses.

I went and spoke to my Director of Programmes. Had he heard of Charles Sobhraj?

"Yes," said John Willis. "The serial killer. What are you doing on him?"

"He's coming to see me," I said casually.

"Oh good. Keep him away from me."

"There might be a programme or two in it," I said.

"Sure." John indicated he was busy.

Serial killers, rapists, druggies, war criminals, fallen angels, big pricks, take-away quizzes – he prided himself on remaining unphased, unenthusiastic. I had cleared the way for Sobhraj to enter the building.

There would be those among my colleagues who would, on political and moral grounds, question my right to meet with a serial killer in the building. They'd want to know if I intended in any way to give him publicity, to glorify his past by exploring it, to offer him money or any other inducement to participate in a programme. He had killed people indiscriminately. For small amounts of money in their wallets, to reclaim the diamonds he'd sold them the day before or just to get hold of their passports against a future contingency. If he wasn't a psychopath, then psychopathy needed redefining.

\*

Sobhraj comes to London and to the Channel 4 offices in Victoria, a proud glass and metal building of the nineties designed by Richard Rogers. He signs the book at reception. My secretary Eva has told the young man and woman there that one Charles Sobhraj, serial killer, is expected to come and see me. They are too young to have followed his exploits in the sixties, seventies and eighties and the books about him were probably out of print when they started to read. They are nevertheless excited.

Eva has told other secretaries on the editorial floor. Some of them have heard of him, or seen, albeit some years previous, the Australian TV serial of his exploits using Art Malik as the star and some of them are fans of the actor. They want a glimpse of him and that's not difficult because our offices are glass cabins with no shelter from scrutiny except screens which can be pulled but always breed suspicion and even attract wolf -whistles.

Sobhraj arrives with a Chinese woman in a smart Parisienne suit. He introduces her as King Ling.

"But you can call her Roseanne which is what the French call her because they don't bother with Chinese." He says this without the least trace of disapproval. That, says his tone, is what the French do.

Sobhraj carries two mobile phones on which he gets calls which King Ling vets and passes to him. They're there to create the effect of being in the thick of some business and preserve the mystery of its nature at the same time by talking in Chinese and in riddling French about seemingly nothing. After the third or fourth call he volunteers to close the phones down for our meeting. He has brought his manuscript.

"What is your literary agent like? Is he good?"

I have thought this one through. The last thing my literary agent wants is to deal with a serial killer.

"She is not taking on any more clients," I say.

"I see, so what are you proposing? Can you get someone?

"I haven't asked him, but I think I have just the person for you," I say.

"I have in mind a friend, a literary agent who has a tough reputation and has sold Indian writers for big money. He is Vikram Seth's agent. "

"Who is Vikram Seth?"

"He is a good writer and this agent got him a lot of money for his second book."

"Why is he good for me?" asks Sobhraj.

"I think you'll approve of him. Let me tell you. I'll call him G."

CS is willing to listen. He sits back with a smile.

"Well G goes to Frankfurt, that's the world's biggest Book Fair where everyone trades books and auctions manuscripts."

"I did not know this."

"Well, he goes with one briefcase and hits the bars where he knows the reps of the big publishing houses all gather for a drink. He finds a seat next to a publishing vulture from London whom he knows to be a princess of the gossip grapevine.

"What have you got for us this year G?" she asks.

"I don't think your firm can afford this one," he says. "This is the big one. Numerous languages, simultaneous rights.. big bucks."

"Yes, but what is it?"

"Confidential."

"But still. I won't tell," she says.

"The Autobiography of Sean Connery – seductions, deals, secrets, rags-to-riches, the lot." He ruffles the thick, titled manuscript in his briefcase and then carefully locks it again using its numbered combination cylinders.

By the time the evening is over G has been invited to every cocktail in town and publishers are looking for him as bees for the only pollinated flower. He goes to his hotel room at one in the morning and calls a number in the USA.

"Mr Connery, you don't know me but my name is G. I am a literary agent. If you want to write your autobiography, I can get you four million dollars," he says.

"From you accent, Mr G you are a fellow Scotsman. I am not about to write my autobiography, but when I do, you can be my agent," says Sean Connery. "That was the story." I sit back.

"I like that man," says Sobhraj. "Eh, what do you think? Roseanne? I want that man. You call him."

I call him. He has heard of Charles Sobhraj and will look at the manuscript the next day when he happens to be in London.

That bit of business done, Sobhraj suggests we have lunch together. We decide on an Indian restaurant and I take him and his Chinese girlfriend, who is very visibly pregnant, to lunch. Very many of the murders he committed were carried out in restaurants in which he would order curry for his victims and poison it. He would openly ask permission to add powders to a guest's curry, telling them that they were organic Indian herbs, the fruit of ancient wisdom, which would disinfect the food and preserve them from amoebic dysentery and the like. The victims would feel the effect of the powders up to twenty-four hours later. They would get diarrhoea. But no problem. Their friend Sobhraj to the rescue. He would acquaint them with his friend, Ajay Chowdhury who lived in the same luxurious complex of flats in Bangkok and would pose as a doctor. Ajay would 'examine' them and Charles, or his then girlfriend Marie-Andre Leclerc, would volunteer to run to the doctor and fetch the supposedly prescribed medicines.

The two of them would give the sick and delirious victims, some of them nauseous beyond caring, strong doses of sleeping pills mixed with lethal chemicals, pretending they were antidotes for the misery they were going through. The pills would put them to sleep and the poisons would kill them. He'd rob them while they were in a coma. He'd now have the money they paid for the diamonds and the diamonds themselves – ready for the next sale, the next murder. And he'd have what money they carried and their passports, which he had cultivated some expertise in doctoring with his own photograph to assume multiple identities.

*

He met these 'guests' of his in planned encounters on the streets of Bangkok. Charles would hang around to see which backpackers went into the Bangkok jewellery shops. He would warn them as they entered that they would be swindled with fake diamonds and jewellery. He would say he could sell them the real thing. Some of them, emerging from the shops, feeling uncertain about the prices and quality of the jewellery they had been shown, would spot Sobhraj and he would, with a 'told-you-so' expression, offer to sell them diamonds, genuine diamonds, very cheap. It would be the first step to ingratiating himself and befriending them.

He had cultivated through his vagrant life a sharp eye for appearances. He'd make sure they were flotsam, back-packers, people who would have, in all likelihood rich families at home but who were content to not be in contact with them for weeks. The relatives back home would eventually find out and perhaps raise the alarm. He calculated he had enough time to cover up his contact with them and make the crimes, even the bodies, untraceable.

So it was that I thought twice before eating a meal with him and I watched his sleeve and my plate with as much clandestine concentration as I could muster. And I watched her too. I kept telling myself that he wanted to sell his manuscript; he didn't need to kill me to do that.

"I have given up all that man," says Sobhraj reading my mind.

"Glad to hear it," I say.

"Now I want to be like you," he says. "I am going to write books like Genet. You know Genet?"

"Not personally."

"He inspires me. And the existentialists."

"I am sure. You must have had plenty of time in Tihar."

"Twenty years, but I kept them busy."

I didn't know whether he meant the years or the jailors.

He was anxious about his book deal. Ten times over the meal he asked how much I thought he could get. I had no idea. He had brought three copies of the manuscript.

I wanted this encounter to come to an end. Would he go? I didn't want him to be hanging around all evening. We could meet the next day to keep our appointment with G. I didn't want to even say I was going home. He might ask where that was.

"We are staying in a hotel in Victoria. A cheap place, owned by some Indian I think because they know who I am and they don't mind."

Always this ambivalence about being a killer and the uncertainty about how famous a killer. Had the reputation, which the Indian press had constructed in the seventies, of the Casanova-Houdini-Hannibal Lector, faded? Who were these Indian landlords and why would they welcome him?

At 53, he is shorter than six foot with very little of a middle age spread, but with a slight tendency to flabbiness. And one could fantasise that his walk and gait were that of a scavenger! There is nothing unusually charismatic about Charles Sobhraj. He wears brown terylene trousers and checked yellow or brown jackets. He could be a ship's cook on a boat registered in Manila.

And that being said, there is something about the eyes which is joyless. Eyes that never smile, even if the mouth grimaces in imitation of humour. He never laughs. Is he the hawk that kills or the hyena that preys on dead flesh? Or both?

\*

G meets him and sees no need for secrecy, introducing himself as Giles Gordon from the Curtis Brown literary agency. After they have a brief conversation, in which Charles boasts about the uniqueness of his memoirs, Giles decides to read the manuscript with a view to representing him.

The manuscript is full of descriptions of how he took over the jail, the bribing with diamonds, the swilling around in excreta, the seduction of a woman lawyer who comes to offer her services to get him out. He seduces her before he tells her that on the contrary he wants to stay in. She is perhaps the first person he tells that he is afraid of being extradited to Bangkok with charges of eleven murders pending against him. The sentence would certainly be death by firing squad. He may even have told her that he committed the crimes and described them. His manuscript, as both Giles and I find out, doesn't say. It cryptically says that they became close, talked a lot and she remains loyal and dedicated to this day.

There is no joy and no relief in the book. It is like Charles himself. It is a relentless story of a man watching his own moves and those of others around him, looking for any breach in their psychological defences through which he can pass to create uncertainty and advantage for himself. It is the banal account of twenty years in a Delhi jail during which he takes control of the prison to the extent that all the jailors, bar the top government-appointed warden and deputies, and even some of them, are in his pay or in his debt; a life in which he creates intrigues about other prisoners and plays games with their lives.

The account, which he has written in his own peculiar pidgin or Franglais, is boastful and imperceptive. It confesses to nothing. It sees his period of incarceration as a series of tiny successive heroisms and tells the story, falsely, as I later find out, of his escape from Tihar, his voluntary 'capture' and return to jail, with an extended sentence – the prize for which he staged the escape.

"Then Fa'ook will write a film," says Sobhraj to Giles. "Or maybe you should write it about me, eh? What you say, man?"

"What about making a documentary in which you tell the truth?" I ask.

"That's too difficult man. But how much will they pay?"

Giles read this manuscript and naturally declined to represent Sobhraj or his writing. Charles, as I observed him, never displayed disappointment or anxiety. Life was a long stride and he took every reverse in it. He didn't ask me to find him another agent. It was as though he had put that project behind him. It was I who brought it up the next time he came to London and got in touch.

"Why don't you write about what you did in Thailand, or even the other experiences you had in jail?"

"What you mean? This is what it is .. this is all about jail in Tihar."

"No it's not. It's all a boast about how you controlled the jail from the start of your term there. You talk about being respected as a top criminal but you say nothing about being a criminal."

"Of course, Fa'ook, there is the whole thing about how I robbed the Jewellery store in the Ashoka hotel."

"Sure, there is all that, but nothing about…. other crimes."

I hesitated before saying 'the serial murders in Bangkok and India and maybe somewhere else?

What Charles was eager to tell me was the truth about his escape from Tihar prison. I had read the accounts in the Indian newspapers and periodicals I picked up in London. Charles could have persisted with the fiction he had foisted on them, but he told me, with a grin, the truth. What he wanted me to appreciate was the fact that he had manipulated the entire Indian media.

# 3

Most accounts of Charles's escape from Tihar jail in 1986, in the books and then in the Bollywood film Charles and Me, tell the story of a cunning and daring escape and then of an unlucky recapture. The same plot is recollected in Shadow of the Cobra.

According to all these, a week before Charles's actual birthday some criminal friends of his, now free ex-jail-mates, drive in to Tihar with a car full of Indian sweetmeats, the sort used for celebrations. These have been laced with generous doses of sleep-inducing drugs. Charles has announced his birthday to all and sundry in the jail and over the years has been hosting parties in his cell and in the Warden's offices where food and celebratory drinks are regularly provided at Charles's expense. On this occasion the sweets are distributed to the Warden, the deputies and the guards at the various gates.

Charles and his accomplices, the guests who have brought them, share the sweets, only partaking of those which are marked as free of the drug. Soon the Warden, deputies and guards are asleep. Charles and his mates take the keys of the jail from their keepers and open the heavy gates. They drive out into Delhi, celebratorily free.

The escape is reported in all the Indian media and represented as a unique and notorious jailbreak. It's big news and the Home Minister himself calls the prison officials to account and issues orders for no effort to be spared to recapture Charles Sobhraj who still has a remainder of his eleven-year sentence to serve, albeit short. A nationwide manhunt is initiated.

Charles ends up in Goa and summons one of his current girlfriends there. The manhunt doesn't succeed, but Charles is, through total coincidence, recognised and arrested by Inspector Madhukar Zende of the Mumbai police, who happened to be in Goa on holiday, in the O'Coqueiro Restaurant in Goa. Charles was sentenced to a further nine years for the crime of escaping from prison.

So the story goes.

What had always puzzled me about this escape story which was so famed all over India was the fairy-tale nature of it. In my mind's eye, I saw a picture of a guarded castle with all the soldiers at the gates and in the courtyards fast asleep. I couldn't recall which fairy story the image or illustration came from, but it was vividly in my imagination. Could all the warders of Tihar jail have been drugged and fallen asleep at the same time? And all of them, including the guards at the gate, in such deep slumber that their keys could be stolen, the succession of gates opened and the celebrity prisoner driven away?

And did Charles politely lock the gates through which he had passed behind him? What was intriguing was that he was the only prisoner to have taken advantage of the opened gates that evening. No other person escaped from Tihar that day?

And wasn't it strange that a police inspector recognised him in a Goa restaurant and arrested him, gaining plaudits and promotions through the lucky encounter?

More than twenty years later I asked Charles about this escape. Chantal was with us when I put the question. Sobhraj grinned. I put the questions to him. Why didn't any other prisoner escape that day? And how could all the warders of the prison be anaesthetised or put to sleep at the same time? Didn't anyone try and stop him?

I can't recall whether it was him or Chantal who told the story. Charles said he had contrived the plot with the drugged sweets to be delivered to the jail and yes, some jail officials did fall asleep as a result and that fact was picked up as he intended. The drugged sweets were his cover for the fact that he had actually bribed the guards who let him escape. Without the drugged sweets story, the guards who let him out would be criminally liable. He was, all those years later, still proud of the fact that the newspapers had swallowed this concocted fantasy.

At the time of the escape, Sobhraj shared his luxury prison wing, equipped with a television set, an electric typewriter, a fridge and a comfortable mattress, with a gentleman called Raj Sethia, a billionaire based initially in the UK, who lost everything though deals and military coups in Africa. He was jailed in India in Tihar and Charles had assisted him by telling him how to use bribery to get accommodated in the 'luxury wing' as a neighbour and friend and one who would share the orders for meals brought in from restaurants in Delhi.

I met Raj after his release from jail when he was a neighbour of my late friend Sadia Dehlavi in Sainik Farms, a select area of Delhi. Raj confirmed the story I had heard from Charles and Chantal about Charles's escape.

Raj said, or hinted at least, that he had provided the funds inside and outside the jail to bribe the guards who let Charles alone out. He knew of Charles's reasons for the 'jailbreak'.

Charles said he got to Goa without anyone recognising or questioning him. He called a girlfriend and went to all the tourist spots and had a good time. He then telephoned a police officer in Mumbai with whom he had, years before, worked a racket in stolen cars. Sobhraj would steal the cars and have them repainted and this officer would hand him false number plates of cars. It was a good trade in the western metropolis.

Charles now asked this officer to immediately take leave and turn up in Goa. He told him where he would be at a particular time on one of the following evenings. The officer should turn up at this designated restaurant and, posing as a dining guest 'recognise' Charles and, despite his protests, arrest him before very many neutral eye-witnesses.

So it was plotted and so it was done.

But why? I asked.

"Because," said Charles, "my prison sentence in India was about to expire in a year's time. India had or still has an extradition treaty with Thailand and after my term expired, the Indian courts would send me back to Thailand to certain conviction for murder and execution by firing squad. But I had read the law of both Thailand and India. India could not extradite me until I had served my full prison sentence for any crimes committed in India itself. And according to Thai law, after 20 years, the murder charge against me would be subject to the statute of limitations, which means it would expire and the case would no longer exist -- so I wouldn't face extradition. I needed nine more years in an Indian prison and, by escaping from Tihar, I got them."

Before he escaped, he told many of his fellow prisoners "see you soon."

They, apart from Raj Sethia, must have wondered what he meant.

# 4

The other episode, related to his connivance to escape being extradited to Thailand and facing capital punishment there, was much more sinister. Charles probably didn't want me to piece together the whole truth and I only gathered the flow of the story in bits and pieces over the months. Later on in our conversations, there would appear a reason for telling me about the escapade, episode, or betrayal. I came to think of it as all three.

In 1994 the Indian armed forces arrested Masood Azhar, a Pakistani terrorist and the secretary of a Pakistan government supported outfit called Harkat-ul-Ansar. Masood travelled to Srinagar under a fake identity, to ease tensions between Harkat-ul-Ansar's feuding factions of Harkat-ul-Jihad-al-Islami and Harkat-ul-Mujahideen. The Indian special forces fought pitched battles with the terrorist outfits in their Kashmiri outposts and succeeded in February in arresting Masood in Khanabal near Anantnag. He was brought to Delhi, charged and convicted as a terrorist and sent to Tihar jail.

As a Pakistani terrorist he was not popular with the thieves, rapists, murderers and other patriotic Indian convicts in the jail and when these had established his identity and come into contact with him in the jail's exercise yard and dining room, they took it upon themselves to demonstrate their love for their motherland by beating him to a pulp. The warders, equally endowed with India patriotism, did nothing to stop the assaults.

Sobhraj, isolated in his luxury wing of the jail, heard screams and shouting from across the yard and asked the jailer outside his wing what it was about. His friendly warder told him that the son-of-a-bitch Pakistani terrorist Masood was getting what was coming to him in the jail's dining hall.

Sobhraj said he never went near the rest of the 'local' convicts, even though his cell wasn't locked and he was free to walk the precincts of the entire jail. He took his exercise in his own time and yard.

This time, though, he walked out of the wing and to the general dining hall, where the shouting was still going on. As he entered the hall from where the warders came and went, the convicts saw him and among murmurs of his name, a silence fell on the dining room. Masood lay on the floor where the others had knocked him down and savagely kicked him. Charles says he ordered the warders to bring the injured Masood to his cell and summon the prison physician or nurse to attend to him. He said he announced to the hushed dining hall that anyone who assaulted Masood would be answerable to him as he believed in the rule of law and courts and not in mob justice even for enemies of the state.

He negotiated with the Warden for Masood to occupy a cell next to his in what he sometimes referred to as the 'private wing' of Tihar. Masood Azhar was badly bruised, internally and externally but recovered in a few days. Sobhraj made sure that he was given a decent mattress and offered to share the food that he and Raj Sethia ordered from restaurants around Delhi for their daily meals.

Masood was obsequiously grateful. He would have undoubtedly have been assaulted again by the patriotic criminals, just as badly, perhaps fatally. The other prisoners, his potential assailants, would have no fear of being held accountable for whatever treatment they meted out. After all he had been convicted of murdering Indian soldiers and civilians and been implicated in plots to bomb and kill and maim innocent Indians. Under Sobhraj's generously offered patronage, he felt safe.

Masood and other invitees would spend time in Charles's cell watching television and would regularly gather to watch the news. One evening the news of army and special forces' raids on terrorists in Kashmir came through. There was footage of the actual assault on terrorist houses and the capture of several of the inhabitants. There was news of other terrorists elsewhere having being killed in an operation that targeted several networks of known terrorists and Pakistani agents operating, as Masood had himself done, in Indian territory.

Masood and Charles, with perhaps some others, watched the news in silence. Masood looked extremely disturbed. It was obvious to Charles that he knew some of the people who had been captured in the collective raids and must have known about the hideouts.

"You know these people?" Charles asked him.

Masood may not have replied, but he looked shaken. They turned to other new bulletins which said that there had been international cooperation in the raids and several agencies had coordinated their efforts. They named the outfits to which the dead and captured terrorists in several countries, belonged. As the news bulletins ended Charles, out of earshot of anyone else, asked Masood if he thought some people he knew or even his friends and relatives could have been targets in these raids. Masood said he was sure they were his people and may have been relatives.

Charles took his mobile phone out of his pocket.

"You can call and find out," he said. "Just dial international, whatever, it will connect you. But do you have the numbers?"

"I know a few in my head, and they will give me all the others," Masood said.

"You can take it into your place, your cell, so no one knows," Charles said.

Masood took the phone and expressed his infinite gratitude.

Three or so hours later, as Charles watched some action drama on TV, Masood returned with the phone.

"It's gone dead."

"Ah, the battery. But did you get through? I can charge it at night and bring it to you again."

"No need," Masood said. He was looking grim.

"Did you make all the calls you needed to?" Charles asked.

"Lots. Enough. It has been disastrous."

Charles expressed his sincere sympathy. I don't know if he said something to the effect of "may their souls rest in peace." Masood must have known that Charles, his friend and benefactor had, like him, sent many to heaven or hell or wherever else their karma had carried them.

They both retired for the night, but Charles shouted for the guards in the early hours of the morning and said he had found himself bleeding. He had cut himself and said he suffered from haemophilia and demanded to be taken immediately to the hospital. There was no prison doctor available, but since he was bent over in agony, he said he would certainly die and the prison would have his blood on its hands if they didn't act on the instant. The deputy warden on duty that night had had very many 'presents' of diamonds and cash from Sobhraj and sanctioned his move to the guarded prison ward of a Delhi hospital. A prisoner's van, rather than an ambulance, carried him there.

Once in the hospital ward, with a junior doctor examining him in bed, Charles sat up and asked to see the senior doctor in charge. The junior wondered what this was about. There was no evidence of haemophilia and the bleeding he had induced had stopped. Charles told him there had been a misunderstanding and he wasn't in pain.

The junior was intrigued.

"Then why did they send you here from Tihar?"

"Because I told them to," Charles said. "Now call the senior person in this hospital. It's a matter of extreme urgency, I want to see Rajiv Gandhi, the Prime Minister."

The junior knew, as did anyone who read the newspapers or watched TV, who Sobhraj was.

He left the room and sent in an administrative official. Sobhraj said it was a matter of national security and he demanded to see the Prime Minister.

The official was intrigued and asked what he could tell the PM's office. Charles said he had information about terrorism and if the official didn't act on his instructions, there would be a disaster and he would have to take the blame. The official was intrigued if not convinced and left the room. He came back some time later and said the hospital had been in touch with the PM's office. The PM wouldn't see him, but some people were being sent to debrief him.

A few hours passed and two men came into the guarded room where Sobhraj was sitting up in bed reading the stack of newspapers he had managed to get hold of. They introduced themselves as members of the Research and Analysis Wing (RAW), the Indian equivalent of the UK's

MI6 or the USA's CIA. What did Sobhraj have to report? Sobhraj said he had nothing to report but he had information vital to anti-terrorism which he was willing to trade in exchange for specific demands from the government of India. The RAW operatives looked at each other.

"So, what's this information you have to give us?"

They didn't at first ask what Charles wanted in return. Perhaps they were waiting to assess the worth of what he had to tell them. He told them that he shared a prison wing with Masood, a name and person with which they were very familiar, and now had procured through Masood more than a score of phone numbers of terrorist contacts. The RAW men must have exchanged glances. In any TV reproduction of the scene, they would.

They left Sobhraj and in a few hours returned to say that they were moving him to a safe house where he would be debriefed. He was still of course a convicted prisoner of the Indian State and would be returned to Tihar afterwards. Sobhraj told them he wasn't bargaining for his freedom from Tihar. He was after something else.

RAW operatives took him from the prison wing of the hospital in a car to a house on the outskirts of Delhi. Sobhraj had his phone with him and the RAW agents asked for it when he recalled the incident of Masood borrowing his phone and calling his terrorist contacts for three or more hours. Sobhraj said he had wiped the memory of all outgoing and even incoming calls from the phone.

"I have memorised the twenty-three numbers which Masood called," he said and grinned. "Now you will have to pull them out of my brain."

"How do we do that?" his RAW interrogator asked.

"In exchange for what I want, I can pour them out," Sobhraj said.

"So, what is it you want?"


Charles told me that he had read in the newspapers that the Indian government was in negotiations with several countries, including Thailand, to modify the treaties covering the extradition of criminals from one country to another. He suspected that if the treaty between Thailand and India was modified, he could be extradited to Thailand before his sentence in India expired, and he would be executed there. In exchange for his vital information, he wanted the Indian Foreign Secretary to make no change to the Thailand-India extradition treaty.

Charles was accommodated comfortably in the 'safe' house and guarded night and day. He was interrogated several times and asked for the phone numbers he said he had memorised. He told them that there were more than twenty traceable calls to India, some to Pakistan and several abroad. He wouldn't hand over even one of them till he was assured that the talks that were in progress between the Indian Foreign Office and other Asian countries had definitely excluded a change in the extradition treaty.

The senior RAW official assured him that his demand had reached the Foreign Ministries' civil servants and asked Charles to fulfil his part of the bargain. That wasn't good enough, Charles said, he wanted the failure of the talks on extradition published in the media and he would then comply.

His phone had been taken from him but, as he said, he had wiped its memory before handing it over. The RAW team doubted his word about having memorised the numbers and were convinced he had written them down and hidden them somewhere. Charles, sharp as ever, knew that this is what they conjectured and agreed to give them one phone number from the bank of those he claimed to have in his memory. They could track that one down and it would prove that he had genuinely valuable information to assist their anti-terror efforts.

He gave them a number and the next day he was told that they had followed the lead, traced the owner of the Sim card and it had led them, as the RAW official put it "to people we are interested in". There was no news from the Foreign Ministry and Charles refused to hand over the rest of the phone numbers.

RAW went into Tihar jail and searched every inch of his room. A warder told them that Sobhraj had, some weeks before he was taken to hospital, asked for a needle and thread kit. He had said he required to stitch back some buttons on his shirt. It was a useful clue. In turning over Charles's cell they found an incompetently or hastily stitched-up tear in the underside of the mattress on his bed. Sure enough, stitched into the mattress was the hastily copied list of phone numbers that Charles had downloaded from the 'recents' in the mobile phone's calls --- Masood's contacts.

Sobhraj was brought back to his cell from the safe house. He noticed his mattress had been replaced and deduced that RAW had found the list of phone numbers, though they said nothing to him. A day after he was returned to his cell the RAW officer, who said he had taken Charles's demand to the Foreign Office, visited him and assured him that whatever the outcome of diplomatic talks, the Foreign Office assured Charles that he would serve his sentence in Tihar and would not be extradited to Thailand.

Masood greeted Charles on his return, asking him how the haemophilia treatment went. He didn't know and never found out about Charles's betrayal. After Charles had served his term and was released and ended up in France, Masood was still in Tihar and still regarded Charles as a friend and ally. They were to communicate in several ways and for several purposes in the ensuing years.

# 5

I am driving Charles Sobhraj to Grantchester, the village near Cambridge which Rupert Brooke made famous in a poem which asks if the vicarage clock will forever stand at half past three and if there will be honey still for tea. On bread or scones, presumably.

Charles is a serial killer. I don't want to call him my friend. How else shall I introduce him? How will John, the person we are going to see, take it? On the phone I tried to explain it without giving away too much, without spelling out the purpose of our mission, while trying to hint that it was important enough for us to be seen.

We are driving down the M11 at a good 85mph in my worse-for-wear black Saab convertible. It is bright autumn weather, about six months after my first encounter with Sobhraj. It's too cold to let the roof down, but pleasant enough to let the breeze into the car with half-lowered windows.

Charles wears half-shades. Part of the persona he has constructed. He has a felt hat and looks like an extra in a spy movie. This is appropriate as we are on a mission of betrayal.

When he called me from Belgium, the day before, he asked me the straight question in his crooked way.

"Fa'ukh, let me ask you this. Do you know anyone in the CIA?"

That was the way he prefaced his questions, testing your willingness or even your eagerness to be drawn into his precious confidence. It was an arrogance he was unaware of.

"How the fuck would I know anyone in the CIA?" I countered.

"I don't know, maybe through television, if they reported something," he said.

"Why the CIA? What do you want with them?"

"I'll tell you later," he said.

After he put the phone down it occurred to me that I did know someone with connections to the CIA. Yes, through my job in TV.

I had lost touch with John Ranelagh over the years. We had been colleagues, commissioning editors in Britain's great TV experiment, Channel 4. Whereas I had been a legitimate commissioning editor, recruited to scout programmes and bring them to the screen, John, it was said, was a plant in the channel by the governing Tories and the personal choice of Mrs Margaret Thatcher, the then Prime minister. Her personal spook in the wheel. While the rest of us had responsibilities perfectly commensurate with the work of a TV station, being editorially responsible for documentaries, films, features etc., John was the "Editor for Northern Ireland and for Chess". The Chess, I am certain, was an unsuccessful cover.

I never found out whether he had been thrust upon the channel and the editorial team by Thatcher or whether our boss had tactfully co-opted him and given him this transparent responsibility in order to appease the Iron Lady. Northern Ireland was on the boil and the Thatcher government had perpetrated the absurd decree that TV stations could not show members of banned and proscribed 'terrorist' – in this case the IRA - organisations or transmit their voices. Their words could be reported but these had to be spoken by actors. John was presumably in charge of seeing that Channel 4 complied.

While working hard at this task, he also held dinners for editors at the Channel to meet Tory Ministers. He lived in Grantchester and occasionally, when he wasn't inclined to go home at night, stayed over in London in his own flat or with the colleague he'd been drinking with and psyching that evening, including myself. We had spent drunken nights together.

He was a mysterious character on one level. Outspoken about his right-wing politics and his hatred of all liberal thought, he was very quiet about the role he was actually playing. To the straight question of whether he was paid by MI6, he would only laugh. About his past too there was some mystery. He had posed as a TV person and been in Zimbabwe when it was still Rhodesia and had, he once let slip, even been given an officer's rank in the Rhodesian army.

He had good contacts with the CIA, so much so that in his time at Channel 4 he was writing a definitive history of that organisation and spent a lot of time in the United States, researching the subject through what he hinted were the most intimate contacts.

"Yes, I do know someone who may have contact with the intelligence, but Charles, I don't want to get pulled any further into this."

He wasn't listening.

"Is it in England?"

"Is what in England?" I asked. I had a feeling of being on a slide I wanted to get off. And yet on the phone I was unable to make my protest any stronger.

"The contact you have?"

"Yes."

"Then you'll see me tomorrow. Keep the day free, man."

He had no rights on my time, no rights to presume I would mobilise my contact for him, but he assumed he had and I knew that my curiosity which had impelled me to listen to him had led me perhaps too far into the business to attempt to withdraw without annoying him. I didn't want to annoy a serial killer. I could introduce him to John Ranelagh and something might come of it. My justification to myself was, as always, that I would turn the material into a story, a film, a documentary, fiction. It was intriguing.

Why did he want any contact with the CIA?

The story of his betrayal of Masood then recurred. I knew that Charles was still in touch with him. Perhaps he wanted to make some sort of deal with the CIA in exchange for information about Masood's terror group? If that was indeed why he wanted contact with the CIA, then Charles was betraying the baddies to the agency that would want to control or eliminate them.

When I had called John, he'd said he'd heard of Charles Sobhraj and yes would be glad to meet him. I said it was possibly a matter that would interest him and would fit in with his ideological convictions and might even result in an international coup in the war of terror. This last would flatter John who thought of himself as a master strategist, albeit an unrecognised one.

There was a frivolous Boy's Own side to John which he was conscious of and didn't bother to hide. Maybe all spooks had to have it. He boasted, hinting that he knew he was being indiscreet, about the missions he had been part of --- the one where in the Rhodesian army he had commanded an execution party which shot four blindfolded terrorists.

John was strange in that he confessed that his family and even his father were sympathisers of the IRA. Was he, from his adolescence in revolt against this family background? He certainly had outspoken right-wing views, spoke with a cultivated English accent and exhibited the prejudices that he thought belonged to the world of the gentleman's club.

There was a side of him which took the business, even the detail of compliance with the State's orders, seriously. There were moments when he became the British Boy Scout or a character out of John Buchan, diligently counting the thirty-nine steps and making sure there weren't thirty-eight.

"Bring him to the house. You've been here before," he said. Then he paused. "Maybe not."

"A pub, suggest a pub."

It was a low-beamed old pub outside Cambridge where John arranged to meet us.

"You know Grantchester? It was where the First World War poet Rupert Brooke lived," I said to Charles as we drove in.

"It must be expensive houses, eh?" he said.

"Yes. But I was telling you about the First World War."

"Yes, they kill a lot of people, eh?"

"A lot of people."

"That's a pity eh?"

"The death of a sparrow is a pity."

He says nothing. Pretends to look at the houses we pass along the way. He is much too sharp to miss my implication, but he gives no sign.

Charles often makes small talk about life and death, looking at a headline in a newspaper, remarking on some accident, an earthquake, a terrorist attack in Jerusalem. He pronounces it "terrible" without the least sense of irony, without a hint in his tone that he himself lives under the shadow of having killed thirty, forty or fifty people for petty gain.

I know that putting a physical distance between myself and Charles will never absolve me. But why am I thinking about absolution? Absolve me from what? I have partnered him in nothing. I don't share the guilt of which he feels none; taken on nothing of his guilt. I didn't know him when he was a murderer. That was twenty and more years ago. He is here with me to make perhaps the only amends he can. He is going to hand over the likes of Osama Bin Laden and perhaps Bin Laden himself, if he knows his whereabouts in Afghanistan or Pakistan, to the American State.

John drinks his dry sherry and wants to impress Charles. He proposes we go to the nearby stables and see his wife's horses being trained, so after a drink we travel to the farm where the horses are. While I watch them being led and watered and put through their paces over the sticks, John and Charles walk into the fields to talk business. Then Charles comes up to me.

"You got me the right man, Fa'ukh. This man know evereeting, even before I talk he know what I'm going to talk."

42

They now go in the farmhouse and he makes some calls on his mobile.

"It will work. Stay cool eh?"

I watch the horses drop pole after pole with their hooves. There are young women riding them and effortlessly urging them to jump, always a few inches short. Maybe it's part of the training routine to urge them to greater heights.

"You've got a dangerous man there," John says to me when they return. The corners of his lips twitch downward. Behind the thick glasses I can see the pupils of his bright eyes. Strangely when he takes his glasses off to rub his eyes or clean his glasses, as he does then, with a corner of his shirt, his eyes shrink, small hooded bird's eyes. He has realised that this is a serious game and not a jaunt, not something to dine out on.

He is now shifty. He wants to be rid of us. He has done what he can, made the initial contacts. He wants no more of it. There's nothing in it for anyone.

"I tell you why I am doing it," I volunteer. Charles is out of earshot. "I want it to end too. I got unnecessarily involved."

"You shouldn't have, old man. This is a deep and dark game."

"You've played some of them," I say looking in his solemn face.

"Stay out of it. leave it to the professionals," he says. His eyes are searching my face.

I answer the implied question.

"Indian connection. I was in college in India with his cousin Raj, though I didn't know that there was any connection between them at the time as he kept it very quiet. I had just read about Sobhraj in the papers. I admit I was fascinated but so was three quarters of India and obviously some in the USA and Australia and the other places from which his victims came. Good TV?"

"Maybe good TV, but bad connection. Not your kind of game, kiddo," he says, usefully.

Charles is full of it on the way back to London.

"Thank you man, you've done it man. They will send someone round to speak with me. I spoke to the big man himself."

"President Bush?"

"No man, the CIA or DSIA fellow in Europe who gather the information."

I didn't ask what the DSIA was.

"I have to change all my phone numbers and give them one. I must buy a number from Woolworths, you know, them cardphone things. Only you will have that number. I won't give it to no-one. I have five phones at present."

I stayed away from his meetings the next day and the day after. He was staying in a hotel in Victoria, a dismal room near the railway station. He phoned me on the third day to say that his 'clients' were putting him up in a proper three-star hotel in a location he couldn't disclose because his 'debriefing' was in progress. If he disappeared for several days on end, I was not to worry.

He disappeared for very many days. For weeks in fact. He phoned me next from Paris. Of course, I was curious to find out what had happened, what deal he had done.

"I am calling on our own secret phone, man," he says. He wants me to feel the intimacy of conspiring. "You want the number eh?"

"I suppose," I say.

He is insensitive to any tone of boredom in his listeners. Nothing puts CS off.

"Everything is fine. I am going to find out where the 'sher' is and tell them and they will do a deal with my lawyers."

"You have lawyers?"

"Not now, but I can get some. You know the top left-wing lawyers in Paris, the fellows who dealt with The Jackal, they volunteer to help me with whatever legal problem I have with the French government. They hate the French government and America more. I never call them, you know, they call me."

"Good, good. So that's it. See you then," I say.

"No, no, no. that's not it. You must have a share. I am asking for good money, some paid later if it succeeds but some straight away. Then I will disappear into America, man. But you will hear from me. I don't give up my friends. You know that."

He had used the word '*sher*', Hindi for lion. I presumed he meant Osama bin Laden. Was that a bluff? --- or perhaps he did have leads through gun-runners to gun-users. I wondered how seriously the CIA would take him.

I was to find out.

*

"So what was the deal with the CIA? Why was he anxious to get in touch with them?" I asked Chantal months later.

"Don't you know? Didn't he tell you?"

"I didn't ask him directly and didn't trust him to tell me the exact truth anyway," I said.

"How about a new identity for him and for me, with American passports and a property in which to live in the United States and pension for life? Would that be a good bargain?"

"Why would they give him and you any of that?"

"In exchange for information?" she said. "Stuff they can't get anywhere else?"

"What sort of information? What has Charles got that they want so desperately that they will do all that?"

"I think I know, but I can't tell you now, Farrukh. Let's just wait and see. He will tell you himself, I think."

# 6

Charles refuses to this day to tell me precisely how he escaped from Thailand in 1975. He maintains that he was unguarded in the police station and simply walked out of it to freedom, worked his way down the coast and got a boat to India. It is almost certain, from his own mealy-mouthed hints, that he bribed one or two Thai policemen or warders to look the other way. After all he still had possession of the diamonds he traded in and the loot he had from his murders.

It is thought that he may have killed a few more people in India. He certainly went to Kathmandu and left a trail of murder which was characteristic of his methods. His victims were never really rich; he seems to have murdered for petty cash and a few passports.

In the months of 1976, traveling all around India in search of victims, he is thought to have murdered a man in Gwalior, in central India. The victim was a Jewish man to whom he had sold some diamonds. Following his pattern of murderous behaviour, he killed the man and then robbed him, retrieving the gems he had sold him. He was arrested for this murder but there was insufficient evidence of his guilt and a court acquitted him.

Charles boasted that he seduced a female Harvard University forensic scientist who had come all the way after reading about his murders in the American newspapers, to volunteer her knowledge and assistance to have him acquitted. The Harvard scientist charmed the provincial Indian judge with her overwhelmingly detailed and contentious testimony on behalf of her lover. He was found not guilty on her expert testimony which contended that the police forensic evidence was stale and unreliable.

When he was telling me he had evaded justice in that case, he made what was an uncharacteristic slip. After explaining that the fellow was a junkie who died of an overdose of heroin and there was no proof as to who had injected him with it, he added, "this fellow deserved to die".

It was in 1977 that his luck eventually ran out and he was jailed for eleven years. Charles told me how it happened.

In Agra, the city of the Taj Mahal, a few hours' drive from Delhi, he and Marie-Andre encountered a coach full of French tourists who were spending their last days in India seeing the Mughal sites of the north.

In the precinct of the Taj Mahal are several shops selling curios, kitsch carvings, models of the Taj, pashmina shawls, authentic and machine-fabricated, and jewellery. The made-up pieces of jewellery, the necklaces, bangles, brooches, rings are mostly in the style of traditional Indian crafts and not quite like the designer jewellery one finds in the West. Infesting these markets and pestering every likely tourist are touts inviting you with the lure of comforts and discounts and the open comparison of the prices which they all claim are the lowest for the best.

Charles and Marie-Andre waited for the tourists to emerge from their sight-seeing of the Taj and were walking in clusters down the Mughal-garden-style fountains that lead to the world heritage marble tomb of the Emperor and Empress. They followed them as they approached the row of shops. Charles had heard some of them say to the touts and to each other, in French, that they would stop by on their way out to buy some gems at these shops, as this was probably their last chance to acquire them before flying back to France the next day.

The protocol of approach was something Charles and Marie-Andre had perfected on the streets and the jewel markets of Bangkok. As some of the Frenchmen and women stopped and were being lured into jewellery shops by their eager and pestering touts, Charles approached them and, speaking in his Parisian French, told them that they were about to be swindled. They'd be sold false gems as the ones they emerge from the shops with won't be the stones they were shown and which they selected. The jewellers who would display them were accomplished sleight-of-hand experts and would show them real emeralds and, right before their eyes, substitute false ones at the point of sale.

A few of the tourists, fascinated at first by this oriental-looking individual who was speaking to them in perfect if colloquially-tainted French, turned to talk to Charles. Marie-Andre with her French-Canadian accent chipped in and after being identified as a Quebequois or whatever, told the now growing assembly that Charles was indeed an honourable and internationally famous gem-dealer.

The tourists were curious and, with some dramatic show of modest reluctance, Charles took out a leather bag of diamonds from his pocket and displayed a few of the stones on a handkerchief on his palm. A couple of the Frenchmen claimed to know about diamonds and could assess their quality, size and worth. Charles asked them to examine his gems. They did, and soon several of the party were asking Charles for the prices and were astounded when he quoted the most reasonable bargains they had encountered in their trip around India.

Charles said he could see from their expressions that they were surprised at the reasonable prices he was asking, but he joked that it was because he had no overheads and never paid any taxes. They appreciated the joke and several of them lined up to buy one or more stones from him. Marie-Andre collected the francs and rupees in their hundreds and thousands.

Of course, Charles and his happy customers began chatting about where they were from, what they had seen in India and where they intended to go now. They said the coach would drive them back to their five-star hotel.

"That must be very expensive," Marie-Andre said.

"Where else can we go? It's our last night and of course none of us want to pay the exorbitant prices the Delhi hotels seem to charge, but what's the option?"

"How many of you?" Charles asked and was given a figure.

"Lemme see, I have a very good friend at the Victory hotel and I think they've just got the right number of rooms. Luxury -- for quarter the price or less. If you want, I can follow you or come with you and take you there and see whether my friend can accommodate you --- I am sure for all this trade he'll even give you a discount – you see I can't take any commission from him." Again, I suppose to make them laugh.

Back in Delhi that evening, the Victory hotel, belonging to a friend of Charles, could accommodate the whole French coachload who settled their bills at their five-star expensive hotel and moved in to spend the night with much expressed gratitude to Sobhraj. They left their luggage in their respective rooms and gathered noisily in the bar where Charles said he and Marie-Andre would wait for them. Marie-Andre took charge of the bar, telling the hotel bartender that she would know the sort of measures and cocktails that the French retinue would order.

Delhi regulations required the bar to shut at midnight. The atmosphere was determinedly boisterous as the entourage wanted a memorable and soaking last night in India. They sang popular French songs and demanded outrageous cocktail mixes from Marie-Andre behind the bar. Close to midnight Charles's plan was implemented. Marie-Andre slipped heavy doses of soporific drugs into the drinks she served. Charles encouraged all of them to have a drink on the house of a special French cocktail he had her make to celebrate their commercial transactions and newfound camaraderie. He calculated that the drug would start working on the victims an hour or so after midnight.

Midnight came and the landlord announced the closure of the bar, saying the police would enforce the regulation, but the raucous party refused to leave.

"Shut the doors, we are staying up drinking all night," they said. Everyone was literally in high spirits. They bundled the hotel owner out of the bar saying they were making him rich by paying for drinks all night.

Charles didn't display his panic. He shut down the music and announced that they all had to go to their rooms as the police would arrest all the revellers after midnight and they wouldn't be able to board their flight the next day. There were shouts in French of 'we'll take the risk' and 'the show goes on'.

The music was turned on again and when Marie-Andre declared the bar closed and turned its lights off, several of the party vaulted over it and began serving whatever was asked for.

Charles didn't know what to do. He attempted to turn the lights out but he was physically restrained. The people who had bought diamonds off him said they'd deal with any intrusion into the party and attempted to get him to enjoy it.

Soon after midnight, one, then two, three, four and more of the revellers succumbed to the strong soporific drug. They collapsed on the dance floor and on the seats. One or two of them were sick. Charles and Marie-Andre saw that the game was about to be up and tried to head for the exit as others were lifting those who had collapsed off the floor and attending to those who were being severely sick as a reaction to the mixture of the sleeping pill and excessive alcohol.

Several of the party who assumed leadership of it were now sure that their drinks had been laced with drugs. The intention was clear.

Charles and Marie-Andre would, through their acquaintance and partnership with the hotel owner or attendants, have had access to the rooms of the drugged and sleeping French party. They would have gone in during the small hours when there was no danger of the victims waking up and retrieved the diamonds they had sold them, perhaps even their passports which they could use in further travels when they needed to change identities and whatever money or valuables they possessed. It would have been a huge haul.

Charles and Marie-Andre were held down by those Frenchmen and women who had not succumbed to the drug and the police were summoned. They were taken into custody, pleading their innocence of this outrageous allegation.

Charles was travelling in India on a passport he had stolen from one of the victims he'd murdered in Thailand. He gave the police the name and nationality on the passport as his own and was the next day, after the facts were investigated by the Delhi police, charged with drugging and attempting to rob the entire collection of French tourists.

As the case proceeded, having drawn the attention of the national press, Charles, from the defendant's box asked to speak to the prosecuting attorney and the judge. His request to so do was granted and he told them that he was not whom his passport said but was Charles Sobhraj and would plead guilty to the charge of attempting to drug and rob the French tourist contingent.

It was a twist in the case. The circumstances and the crime remained the same, only the motivation for Charles's admission as to his real identity was not immediately apparent to the court. Why was he confessing to being an alleged fugitive murderer?

Nevertheless, the entire story of the drugging of the French tourists in the bar of the Victory hotel and the deduced intention to rob them of the diamonds which he had sold them and any other possessions he and his lady accomplice could lay their hands on, was rehearsed by witnesses in court. The French contingent, or at least some of them, were kept back from returning to France and gave evidence in the case in the following weeks.

Both Sobhraj and Marie-Andre were convicted and sent to separate jails. Charles boasted to me that he courted the sentence and that he had actually taken the trouble to read the statutes of Indian law and the treaties under which he could be extradited to Thailand. He discovered that Indian law required anyone convicted of a crime in India to serve their sentence or endure whatever punishment the court ordered before they could be sent under extradition law to any other country. He realised that this was a way of escaping the death sentence he would face in Thailand.

The Delhi High court awarded him eleven of the twenty-year period of detention he sought. This was 1977 and the beginning of his stay in Tihar, from which he escaped and contrived to have himself recaptured in order to get the additional years he needed in an Indian jail.

# 7

Eventually, not as the result of any acquittal, but because he had served his twenty-year sentence, Sobhraj was released from Tihar in February 1997.

His release was international news. Richard Neville, his accusative biographer, faced him in a TV studio. Neville put it to him that he had confessed to the murders years before, when the chances of his ever being released seemed remote. Sobhraj was cocky and defiant. He had done no such thing. Neville could say what he liked, but he had no proof. He, Sobhraj, had been very careful. Whatever people thought, he couldn't be convicted in a court of law because there was no evidence. He never said he was innocent, but insisted that he had never been convicted of murder and would sue anyone who said he was guilty of it.

It was a cocky performance. The one thing it lacked was any knowledge of his audience. Since Charles Sobhraj was incarcerated in 1976, the world had moved on.

His legalistic contentions came across as the bragging of an unrepentant killer.

He said he was off to France.

*

It was not to be, at least not then. Sobhraj was immediately arrested again in February 1997 and the Indian police, working diligently with their files, were attempting to charge him with what they were sure were murders he had committed before he went into Tihar.

Then, according to Charles, fate took a hand in his fortunes. Some French students touring India had landed up in the sunny and watery resorts of Kerala and had come upon the Thorium-refining plants in that territory, used by the Indian armed forces as fuel for nuclear bombs. The enclosures of these plants were treated as forbidden territory. The French gang, being engineering students, photographed the facility and were apprehended by the Kerala police doing it. The photographs were declared the work of Pakistani spies targeting India's nuclear installations and plants. The story was all over the media.

The French students were arrested and would be tried as spies. They were no such thing. They were careless young people taking random photographs on their travels to show to their friends in France and boast that they had pictures of India's nuclear capabilities, albeit from across a bevy of barbed wire fences.

The French ambassador argued their case with the Indian Home Minister who concurred with the opinion that these were foolish young people and not Pakistani spies. The Indian government made a deal. They would release the French students if France would accept the nuisance Sobhraj as well, as he had originally travelled on a French passport and was indeed a French citizen.

The deal was struck and Charles Sobhraj, whose real name was and is Gurumukh Bhavnani, the name and surname bestowed on him at birth by his Sindhi father, Sobhraj Bhavnani, flew to France.

*

In the small hours of the morning in a house in New England USA watching, on CNN, the TV interview with Richard Neville on Charles's release is one Chantal Harris nee Compagnon. She sits in her dressing gown in the downstairs drawing room of the house she shares with her husband and two daughters, both in their twenties. Chantal is forty something. She has left the conjugal bed and fetched herself a coffee from the kitchen. She turns the volume of the TV really low. She doesn't want to disturb her husband or wake her two daughters, each in her own bedroom upstairs.

Her 'Indian' daughter, Usha, is a light sleeper. She comes out of her room and sees the faint blue light beyond the well of the stairs. She comes down the stairs rubbing her eyes.

"What are you doing mum?"

"I couldn't sleep, so I just turned on the telly," Chantal replies, switching the TV off through the remote control.

Usha takes one look at her mother and knows that she looks guilty, she is lying. She takes the remote control and turns the TV on. Standing behind the sofa on which Chantal sits, Usha looks at the screen and the programme her mum was watching. There's a man being interviewed. He says he may or may not have committed the murders that the interviewer accuses him of, but he doesn't want to say.

"I don't want to say I did it or I did not do it, because it would ruin my commercialite," he says, accenting the final 'e' as in French. He smiles implying to the interviewer that that should explain it all, they should understand each other.

Chantal watches transfixed but nervous at Usha viewing the same thing.

"What is this mother?" Usha asks.

"Some news," Chantal replies.

"Why are you watching news about a killer. He looks a horrible man."

Chantal doesn't reply. Instead she grabs the remote from Usha to turn the picture off or over. Usha grabs it back. What's her mum afraid of?

"I must see this," Usha says.

There must be something in Chantal's frenzy that tells Usha more than what Chantal is willing to admit.

She is intuitively suspicious. Usha senses that there is a play of personal history in the room. This is no ordinary night, no ordinary CNN bulletin, no ordinary idle insomnia. She looks in her mother's face. There is a terrible discovery there, a terrible confession, a melting of emotion that has hardened these twenty-seven or so years.

Usha has always been told by her mother and by Mr Harris whom she regards as her father that her natural father is an Indian but that he abandoned her and Chantal and has never been heard of since. She has always accepted the story and has treated Mr Harris with all her heart as her real father, her only father, the only one she wants and needs. And Mr Harris, in turn, has treated her like his own child in every respect, even when his own daughter comes along, two years younger than Usha and the perfect sister for her, completing the neat family of Harris the landscape gardener and Mrs Harris the housewife and part-time translator of French documents for an agency.

Now in her mother's face the years dissolve. There is some vivid recollection playing through her mind and perhaps some longing and even some fear. Usha knows that her mother hasn't seen this man who is on the screen for years but that she has seen him. She knows him. Her heartbeat tells her that she knows him intimately.

58

On screen, the man is defiantly saying that he is a 'top criminal' and that's why people in and out of jail all over the world respect him. The interviewer tries to remind him of something called morality, that there are judgements of good and bad behaviour that prevail and ought to prevail in the world, above considerations of 'top' criminality. The man thinks that's funny.

Usha looks in her mother's eyes and holds her by the shoulders.

"You know this man, don't you?"

"Which man?" Chantal pretends to not understand the question. But the act is not convincing, there is no effort in it. She is beyond wanting to preserve the secret. There is an inclination in her to wake the house with it but she suppresses it and Usha can sense, smell, the conflict in her mother's sweating breast.

"I don't believe this," the young girl says. "I don't believe it."

The tears are welling up in her eyes, through shock rather than sadness.

"Tell me no, you can't have!"

Chantal looks on helpless, speechless.

"That's my father isn't it?"

Chantal doesn't deny it and Usha screams and runs into the Connecticut night. Mr Harris and the younger daughter Safrine wake up and rush down the stairs. The programme is over. Chantal says Usha's gone and Mr Harris, gathering what he can, runs out after her. She has taken her car.

Harris comes back two hours later after trying to track her down on his own. Chantal is packed and ready to leave by then. He knows where she is going. He clings to Safrine and cries. He is beyond caring what he says. He is a good man, a landscape gardener (or so the reports call him, though Chantal said he was an academic) by profession and a would-be writer.

He rescued Chantal from penury on the streets of Kabul when she emerged from jail, having been abandoned by Sobhraj after the pair of them had been sentenced to six months each for stealing a car and attempting to cross the border to Pakistan in it. They had each been sent to different prisons, Sobhraj to the male prison and Chantal to the female. In a few days he escaped and promptly left Kabul. There was, he said, no way he could hang around or get word to her so he abandoned her and made for Bombay, for other adventures.

Six months later she emerged from jail without any money or possessions. She had, thank providence, entrusted her child to her parents in Paris but was longing to be reunited with her. Mr Harris was a hippy on the trail and he assisted Chantal (and later adopted Usha who was retrieved by Chantal from her parents in France) and induced her to apply for a divorce from her errant husband -- Yes, he had married her two years previous to their Kabul exploit – and to marry him and move to the States.

For years, bringing up the two girls, she thought she had made the right choice. She followed the adventures of one Charles Sobhraj in the newspapers and later in the books written by Richard Neville and by Thomas Thompson, knowing how much of the latter was fiction. She told me she followed Charles's life in jail, the escape and recapture. She never said whether her husband or daughters knew that she was still pining for him.

He had, as far as she could personally testify, only killed one man when she had been with him. That was the Pakistani taxi driver whose car they stole and who died when he was tied up and crammed for a few hundred miles in the boot of his own car. Apart from that death, which she thinks to this day was unfortunate but not intentional murder, she didn't know or want to believe the accounts in books of the other spiral of murders. Or so she said. She was convinced that Sobhraj didn't go for guns and crimes related to violence. But was the death cult he represented in person a subconscious attraction?

Did she admit to herself when she took the decision to return that, since he had abandoned her and she had left for a new life in the USA, he had gone berserk. He had set up in Thailand, paired up with a succession of adoring and pliable women and with them committed the most awful murders. When she spoke to me about Marie-Andre, Chantal seemed convinced that it was Marie-Andre who had initiated the murders and theft. Or so she said.

 She also blamed Ajay, calling him the real homicidal psychopath who actually committed the crimes which Charles perhaps became embroiled in. Charles wasn't the hawk, merely the hyena --- which is what she implied in defence of him --- but in her eyes and through her actions I could see that her fascination was for the hawk who had an uncaring command over the life and death of creatures, even if there was mixed into that pride, the shame of tolerating the lowly scavenger who preyed on the dead.

*

Charles called me from Paris.

"My wife is back and we are going to live together. She will handle the book and all the film affairs."

"I thought you were with King Ling -- Roseanne. And you have a baby girl with her, n'est ce pas?"

"Yes, but my wife doesn't know that and Roseanne doesn't know that Chantal has come back all the way from the States to join me. So, don't say nothing, OK, ole man?"

I meet Chantal when Sobhraj brings her on his next trip to London. He says he is willing to make a documentary or even a documentary series if they will pay him and he is willing to be debriefed by me for a screenplay, again if he is adequately paid for his pains.

She is, I guess, nearly fifty years old. She has a charming broad smile and must have been a French beauty in that sixties genre that Truffaut and Chabrol made popular. Her father owns property near the French Alps. She also says she has about fifty thousand pounds which she is going to invest in a business with Charles. Charles asks me to keep her occupied and he disappears for a half hour at a time to phone Roseanne in Paris.

Chantal is full of the promise of a new life with her original love. She knows it will be hard but she wouldn't have abandoned Mr Harris and her family and the States if she didn't know this was what she wanted. This man was the love of her life and her destiny. Perhaps in her heart she knew he was a killer and without any means to plumb those depths, one may speculate that this was the lode stone in the field of attraction.

There were relatives of the victims – if he had murdered so many ---out there who would try and get their revenge. She was aware of that.

Some of the things she said to me indicated that she would get him to regret what he had done because she had noticed, as I said I had, that there was no sense of regret or repentance for the murders and misery he had caused. She said if it were true that he had murdered all these people under the influence of Ajay and Marie-Andre, she could understand the misery he had caused very well. Sometimes in our conversations, her tone and expression were of genuine concern.

But surely Sobhraj was a psychopath? Because he couldn't put himself imaginatively in the place of his victims or of those to whom he had caused suffering? She was convinced he was not. That he had done these things out of the force of necessity at the time and the really psychopathic killings were not his work but that of Ajay and the women. She was sure. She knew her man.

"And you aren't scared of him, even with your fifty thousand pounds and your cheque book?"

"No," she said laughing it off and then, "You are getting to know him, Farrukh, do you think I should be?"

# 8.

Chantal said she was waiting in a car in Paris for Charles outside the prison on the day in 1969 when he was due to be released. He had served his sentence for stealing cars from the streets of the city.

He had arrived and lived in Paris with his mother who had married a French soldier serving in Vietnam after his birth father abandoned them and went back to India.

According to Chantal, she and Charles got married soon after his release from jail and she got pregnant. The day that they got married, Charles was again arrested by the French police. He was charged under a complaint from his half-sister whose signature he had forged and from whom he had stolen thousands of francs. Chantal approached the sister to drop the charges and after a lot of argument and recrimination, she agreed and Charles was released.

He didn't go straight but was again about to be apprehended for forgery when he persuaded Chantal to leave France with him and travel to India, where his Indian father, called Sobhraj Bhavnani, though a frequent international traveller, was based.

They crossed Europe and Asia minor by car and ended up in Bombay. They lived in a small flat and their daughter Usha was born. Charles's father, whom the books persist in calling 'Hotchand Sobhraj', though neither Charles nor Chantal ever used that name when speaking of him to me, was probably back in Vietnam at the time on business.

In Bombay, Charles began to steal fancy cars and take them from one city to another, changing the colours and the number plates, acquiring false documents through acquaintance with corrupt Bombay policemen, and selling them for tidy sums. My friend, the legendary Hindi film and TV serial actor Sanjay Khan, recalls the time he was approached by Sobhraj with a proposal to buy a fancy European car, a rare 'breed'. The deal came to nothing as Sanjay said he was wary of the fellow and suspected the car was not quite his to sell.

Charles and Chantal went on to Delhi where Charles pulled what became a notorious and well-chronicled robbery. The published accounts of the robbery say that Charles and an accomplice surveyed Delhi's Asoka hotel where a jewellery shop in the hotel's shopping arcade was situated directly below a guest room on the first floor. The occupant of the room above the shop was a flamenco dancer and the reports of the robbery say that Sobhraj and his accomplice held her hostage for three days in her room while they found a way to drill a hole in the floor of the room through which they could access the jewellery shop below at night without setting off burglar alarms and escape with all the display in the cabinets.

As he recalls those days to me, now in 1998, Charles throws back his head and says that's what he planned for the press and other gullible idiots. He had constantly visited the Asoka and struck up a conversation, then an acquaintanceship and then a romance with the Flamenco dancer. He didn't need to hold her hostage in her room. She invited him to it and he used this friendly access to, in a few hours of one night, rather than the three of the reports that they put out, drill through the floor to the jewellery shop.

She had to tell the hotel and the Delhi police that she was held hostage and wasn't complicit in any way in the plan. He even bragged that the hotel staff at the time were very busy paying fawning attention to Henry Kissinger who was lodged there on a diplomatic visit to the Indian capital.

Sobhraj didn't get away with it. He was caught and convicted for the robbery.

For the first but not the only time, according to Charles's recollection, he feigned a burst appendix and was taken to the prisoners' wing of a public hospital from where he contrived to escape.

Charles was very proud of all his escapes, in Greece, in Iran and elsewhere. He liked to think of himself as the Houdini of jailbreaks; they presented him in a heroic light and the media fell for it. The only story that I remember clearly was his debunking of the sleeping-pill fabrication in Tihar.

It may be that I encountered Raj Sethia before I put the question of the improbability of the drugged birthday sweets to Charles. I can't place the sequence in time, but I remember Raj telling me that he fixed for payments on behalf of Charles. Admitting to bribing the guards to get hold of the keys was uncharacteristic. For decades he had basked in the fabricated ingenuity of his escape.

Having escaped from jail for the Asoka hotel robbery, he told Chantal that they had to get out of India. They would go via Pakistan to Afghanistan. Chantal said she wanted to stay with Charles, but there was the one-year-old Usha to consider. She decided to send Usha, in the care of a friend who was flying to Paris, to her committed Catholic parents who would look after her. With the baby dispatched, Charles and Chantal set off, driving to Afghanistan.

There are conflicting accounts of this escapade in the life and crimes of Charles Sobhraj. After a few weeks in Kandahar and Kabul, Charles and Chantal were both arrested by the Afghan police.

According to Charles the arrests were for some minor misdemeanour such as not having the right papers for the car they were driving as it had a foreign numberplate. It is more than likely that the Kabul police and their special branch were alerted to much more serious offences. It may even be that they were suspects in the murder of some back-packer whom Charles had robbed of his passport and money. The threat of their arrest and conviction was serious enough for them to decide to leave the country, driving to Herat and then crossing the border to Iran.

And here's where the account that Charles gives to Richard Neville and Julie Clarke differs from what Chantal told me.

According to her, on their way to Afghanistan, they hired a Pakistani car and its driver who drove them to the Khyber Pass, the Afghan border. The driver said he wasn't going any further. He wanted to return to his family and besides, he didn't have a visa to enter Afghanistan or take his car through. They should take a bus or find some other way to get to where they wanted to go.

Charles agreed to turn back but when they stopped for a cup of tea on the highway, he poisoned the driver's drink and when he passed out, stuffed him into the boot of the car and turned back. When they got to a lone spot Charles, driving the car, stopped and opened the boot. The driver was dead. Chantal said she hadn't participated in the murder, but now Charles asked her to help him dump and destroy the body. They may have poured petrol over it and burnt it. The body was never discovered and the driver has gone down in the police records as a missing person.

At any rate they moved on and got to Kabul. As they were fleeing the city, intending to cross over to Iran, they were followed by the Afghan police and taken back to Kabul where they were convicted of offences which didn't merit long sentences, such as not registering a foreign-plated car, and sent to different prisons – Charles to the men's jail and Chantal to the Afghan women's.

Charles bribed his way out of the men's jail and says he was smuggled by some French tourists whose help he solicited and crossed the border to Iran and thence to Pakistan.

According to the account he gave Neville and Clarke, his obsession was now to get back to Kabul and contrive a way of freeing Chantal. In their book he says he made his way to Paris and brought his daughter, the one-year-old Usha, whom the book calls 'Madhu', back with him. He hires a nurse to look after her and on the way through Pakistan to Kabul he picks up a young traveller on the hippy trail called Diana. This girl is happy to ride with him. The murder of the Pakistani driver now takes place on this journey.

The book, based on the 'confessions' of Charles, outlines the horror of Charles drugging the thirty-something Pakistani driver in the presence of Diana, with 'Madhu' and the nurse asleep in the back of the car. He stows the body in the boot of the car and when he reaches an isolated spot, opens the boot to a nasty smell of human excreta. The boot of the car was not air tight, so the driver couldn't have suffocated, but must have suffered a heart attack. Diana witnesses this scene as she, defying Charles's instruction to stay put, steps out of the car. He asks her to help him dispose of the body, luring her into complicity in manslaughter.

They get rid of the body and drive on towards Kabul where Charles says he plans to convince Diana to commit some offence and have herself arrested and sent to the women's prison and get in touch with Chantal and outline a plan to escape through an underground tunnel which Charles would dig from the outside of the prison.

None of this happens. According to the book, Diana informs the Pakistani police about the murder of the driver. Chantal doesn't escape from the Kabul women's prison through the tunnel but is released after serving her sentence.

She forms her partnership with the American and Chantal returns with him to the US, settles down with him, fetching Usha from her parents in Paris and subsequently has another daughter by this Mr Harris.

Sobhraj meanwhile has been in Bangkok, escaped execution for the murders which Herman Kippenberg meticulously detected and exposed, has landed up in India, been arrested for poisoning the group of French tourists with intent to rob them and has contrived to stay in an Indian jail until the statute of limitations in Thai law brings an end to his conviction and sentence of capital punishment for the murders on Thai soil.

\*

When Chantal joins him in Paris in 1997, he lodges her in cheap hotels and stays with her occasionally, making trips, presumably to his Chinese family, leaving his absences from Chantal a mystery in which she colludes. She asks no questions and is probably told very many lies.

After Chantal's return to Paris and her introduction to me in London, I receive a phone call from the US in my office at Channel 4. I remember the caller introducing himself as Harris. He says he is Chantal's abandoned husband and asks me if I am responsible for housing Sobhraj and Chantal and paying for their upkeep. He is polite and extremely decent in his enquiries despite the distress and antagonism he must feel. I assure him that I don't regard Sobhraj as a 'friend', am perfectly aware of his reputation as a serial killer and that I am not in any way housing or indulging or bank-rolling him. I wonder what Mr Harris wants me to say or do. He rings off after saying he is sorry to have troubled me and won't bother me again.

# 9

Through several meetings and phone calls, I get the feeling that Chantal, having sacrificed everything she had had for the last twenty and more years, including two daughters and a devoted husband, has returned to an uncertain future with Charles in Paris. What was the source of the attraction that compelled her to do it?

Perhaps a psychologist or psycho-analyst can say why women fall for, offer sex to and want to marry murderers on death row. What attracted women to Charles Sobhraj? Throughout my acquaintance with Charles I asked myself this question and will ask it again and again in this memoir.

I never detected, even as a completely objective observer, any trait of male attractiveness that one could perhaps see in pop stars, iconic actors, politicians of power, men with an incredible sense of humour, James-Bondish good looks, dynamic intelligence and compelling creativity – perhaps even just compelling style of dress and bearing. I couldn't see any of these in Sobhraj. He wasn't a great conversationalist and had no cultural or artistic allure. I also know and read of women who are attracted to money and put up with decrepit old men to get their hands on it. Sobhraj for all his dealings was broke.

Then what was it that, according to the reports written about him and according to his own boasts, brought women to offer themselves to him? Was it the allure of someone who had in a sense assumed a power over life and death? The actual modus operandi of the murders was not valiant but cowardly and disgusting.

Chantal would be the perfect person to answer the question, but was she capable? Did she know why she was back in Paris in pursuit of him? I never put the question to her because I was aware that the only answer she was capable of, however insightful she was about anything else, was "I love him". But what I imagined, rightly or wrongly, was that Chantal harboured some twisted instinct of motherhood, or protectiveness towards a ruined boy.

Charles didn't treat Chantal too well on her return. She didn't return to her relatives --- she never referred to them in my presence – or to her friends' houses, but lived in seedy hotels and saw Charles when he would condescend to see her. Did she know about Roseanne and the child? How could she not?

It was Chantal who told me that Charles had agreed that she would divorce her husband in the US and they would remarry. It was, in her mind, their guarantee of a future. She had no money and no source of income. She lived off her credit cards and ran up debts, perhaps running away from the boarding house hotels without settling her bills.

In December 1998, something provoked her to leave Paris and leave Charles. I didn't know when or why, but he called me and said Chantal had quit Paris after they quarreled and would I please call her on the mobile number he gave me, as she wasn't answering his calls, even though he called from different phones. He pleaded with me to ask her to return. I was reluctant to intervene in what was none of my business but I had already been told bits and pieces of the Charles saga and if I was to make anything of it, Chantal would be a key source. I called her and merely said Charles had been in touch with me and wanted her to return from wherever she was to him.

She thanked me for the call and said she would write me a letter and asked where she should send it. I had been reluctant since I met him to give Charles any indication of where I and my family lived, but I gave Chantal a postal address.

She wrote to me :

*Wed Dec 16 '98*

*Farrukh, I can't stand the <u>VOID</u> I am in… I is like being between life and death… as I was deprived of the most elementary breath……*


*Dearest Farrukh,*


*Thanks for your phone call___ And yes, you're right: I should and will stay in touch with Charles, as if everything was peachy and rosy, as it would be the easiest way to get things happening both for the BBC deal and the movie this in Soli's and your presence. After all, officially I am still Charles' wife-to-be. Which by the way, is something you might be able to mention in your discussion with the BBC folks or whoever: the "wife-to-be" bit might come in handy for contractual purposes….*

*As I told you over the phone, Charles has offered to pick me up from wherever I might be at that time, to bring me to London with him (2nd week of January?). I have not told him yet about my being in Barcelona early January, but I will most probably have to as he is supposed to pick me up – or I'll meet him in Paris, after having come up from the South by train, and both of us will go to London. I'll keep you posted closely.*

(She then gives me at some length her Barcelona phone numbers and dates and says her French mobile will be on and available)

*I will stay at my girls' godmother's place, who lived in India for many years and has adopted a beautiful little girl from South India_ (She is a real lover of India).*

*Anyway, my dear friend thank you again for your support – and let us stay in close touch, please!*

*Best wishes,*

*Chantal*

*P.S. I sent Charles photocopies of my bills....! Awaiting reaction.*

Chantal obviously doesn't require a response from me as she doesn't put an address on her letter. She doesn't have an address. Charles seems to have set her adrift. She gives me her travel plans for no particular reason. The 'Soli' she alludes to is my then agent for Indian journalistic assignments, a friend and film producer – but more of him in the next chapter

# 10

It's almost midnight and my phone rings.

"Fa'ook, this is Charles, I need your help."

"It's midnight where are you? What help?"

"Yeah, exactly, I am in London. Can you come?"

"Come where? What's happening?"

"I am in the Victoria Casino and need some money to get my car out of the car park. I lost everything, see, and I can't leave this place. Chantal is with me."

It sinks in. The addictive gambler has lost every penny in some casino and hasn't enough left to get his car out of the park. Obviously neither he nor Chantal have debit or credit cards that work, though they must have possession of tens of them if not hundreds."

"Where is the Victoria Casino?" I ask.

"In Edgware Road," Chantal, to whom the phone has been transferred, says. "Can you please come quickly, Farrukh. Sorry for this bother, really but there's no one else we could ask."

The image of the casino's sign which I may have passed a thousand times without noticing, flashed up. Yes, I knew where it was, on the right a few hundred yards up from Marble Arch.

"I know it. Right, I'll see you there."

"Can you bring cash?" Chantal says. "Is about 30 pounds to get out of the park."

They must have parked the car that morning or afternoon and been gambling in the casino since.

I told my partner Margaret that I was going to rescue Sobhraj and Chantal from some joint and I'd be back straight after. She said she'd come for the ride, just to keep me company. I checked my wallet and bank cards and we set out from South London. The drive would take about 40 minutes at that time of night.

Edgware Road, home to the expat and visiting Arab community of London was still alive with its Arab restaurants and even the grocery shops with trestles of fruit and vegetables still open and buzzing – an oasis in the slumbering desert of residential London through which we drove.

I parked the car in a square through a side street and walked back to the main road. I looked for a hole in the wall cash dispenser and took out the thirty pounds they said they needed.

We found the entrance to the Victoria. I'd never been into a casino, not in London, Goa or Monte Carlo, but had seen a hundred interiors in films, where the clients in evening dress push gambling chips across tables and croupiers keep poker faces. So I thought I knew what to expect.

The Victoria wasn't anything like that. We went up the dark and dusty staircase and through a lobby of fruit machines where one or two shabbily dressed clientele were pushing coins and pulling the lever of the one-armed bandits – or perhaps they were pressing electronic buttons to make the fruit discs spin.

The hall was just as shabby with a coffee counter or bar at one end and tables full of gamblers who didn't resemble 007 in the least. The whole place looked sad, depressing, a vale of losers. Was this casino an exception? Were they all like this? Did the films dress up Mr Hyde to look like Dr Jekyll? Probably not. The Victoria, a commercial casino without the need to maintain the stiff upper lip of a luxury hotel or the flash of Las Vegas or the Riviera, seemed to me the downmarket version for the hopelessly hopeful.

I spotted Charles and Chantal. He was wearing the light brown tweedish jacket I had seen him in before. Chantal's designer dress looked crumpled. She may have slept in it the previous night.

"Thank you," they both said.

They didn't seem anxious to get away. I handed Charles the money.

"I'll get the car from the basement and see you in the street," Charles said.

Chantal looked exhausted. She said we should walk down and wait for him. She didn't volunteer any information about how they'd got there or when or why. I didn't ask.

We waited in the street.

"Everything, he lost everything. He would have sold me if he could," Chantal said when she joined us. There was no bitterness in her tone. She didn't say how or why they were in London.

We walked to the square where my car was parked with Charles following us in his cream coloured, battered old Mercedes. They'd driven here from Paris.

"Old man," Charles said as we stood between our cars. "You have to lend me some money. We have to pay for the ferry across from Dover to Calais."

"How much will that be?" I asked. "My debit card has a limit."

"You have a credit card also?" Charles said.

I did.

"Just lend me the money, about six hundred and when I get to Paris, I will just send it back to you."

I didn't think I had an option.

We walked to the cash dispenser and I pulled out the required amount using both my cards. Chantal assured me that the money would be returned immediately they reached Paris and she said she was sorry.

"We'll drive to Dover now and sleep in the car," she said.

"The ferries probably run all night," I said.

It was two o'clock and we went our ways.

It was years later that Chantal told me how and why they'd got to the Victoria casino that night.

*

Very curiously, she wrote me a letter, perhaps sitting in the car that morning.

The postage was French so she sent it when they reached Paris the next day.

She wrote the four pages as she says at the top of the letter *"On the way to Dover."*

*Tues Feb 2 '99*

*Dearest Farrukh*

*A quick note as Charles and I are hitting the road back to France – from the car – I am going back to Barcelona and*

*Charles to Paris, until we come back together to London –
hopefully in a couple of weeks – to await Soli's arrival.*

*I am really sorry not to have seen you during our short
stay in London. I wish I could have met you last Thursday,
when I tried reaching you late afternoon, to spend a little
while with you. But….*

*Charles and I have talked at great length after not having
been together for over three months and he seems well
intentioned towards settling or rather dealing with my
credit card debts etc. The fact is that we are supposed to
be building a life together and give it a big chance this
time – so the movie deal and the BBC project should give
us/me the ability to take care of financial matters and we
could start doing just that when Soli arrives with the funds.
The plan is that as soon as you inform us of his arrival
date in London, we will come back here together – most
probably a couple of days ahead –*

*Could you inform us <u>individually</u> of that date, so that I
can make my travel plans from Barcelona adequately to
join Charles (Thanks).*

(She then writes three phone numbers and an e-mail where
she can be reached)

*Now Farrukh! I must tell you that I really fancy the idea of
living in London as I get a better feel for the city now and
am quite comfortable moving around it. And so does
Charles. In fact we really want to get a flat here. So we
will look into that next time we are in town, for sure.*

*In the meantime would you be able to provide me with
some leads for <u>work</u> (for myself)?*

*I am anxious to get back into working and to do things I
used to do and like to do. Do you think it would be
possible for me to find anything? In production maybe, as*

79

*that's what I used to do (freelance and for groups) in the music biz? Or in anything you think I would fit in? Maybe start looking into temp work? What do you suggest? – As far as freelance work might be conceived, I will be equipped with a good laptop again as soon as money comes in. My Mac is out of commission for good this time.*

*Charles spoke with Tom Roberts and it sounds like James Marsh is a creative and interesting director. Apparently, he is still in the US but will want to meet with Charles as soon as he gets back. Maybe when we are in London in the next two or three weeks? In all it seems like the BBC project could be an interesting one. And Charles agrees that having my name on the contract is a good idea. So, Farrukh, I'll be an artistic consultant for the project, if possible!! (?) I would love to.*

*Please e-mail me your thoughts when you have a chance. I can't wait to get back to work….*

*Best wishes always, Love,*

*Chantal*

*P.S. I'll fill you in on the Charles/Chantal saga*

*P.S 2. Please forgive the messy handwriting! not too easy in a moving vehicle.*

*P.S 3 I just remembered that when we spent that evening in Paris in late October you had mentioned something about the possibility of renting flats with an option to buy, in other words, after some down payment, rent money becomes mortgage money. Is that correct, Farrukh? If that's the case that might be a smart way to go for us/for me/for anybody*

What was clear from her letter to me was that they had spent longer than the previous day in London. What was Charles doing apart from losing money in the casino?

Chantal's interest in a London flat and moving to the city seemed to me an attempt to get away from Paris and put some distance between Charles and Roseanne and their daughter. The letter made me wonder how Charles and Chantal survived, financially. They obviously didn't have credit or debit cards with which they could extract their vehicle from the car park or pay for the ferry back to France. And where did he get the money he gambled away at the Victoria Casino?

It was months later, through Chantal, that I was to find out.

\*

Her family owned some land on the border between France and Switzerland and her father had transferred it into her name. Charles said he wanted to survey it to see what they could do with it but once there, he said they were never going to settle there and grow turnips or whatever, so the best thing they could do would be to sell it. If I remember correctly, she said they went to an estate dealer and sold the piece of land for forty thousand pounds.

Charles said that to celebrate they would take a holiday in Amsterdam so that's where they drove. They booked into a hotel in Amsterdam and Charles said they should go to a casino as he felt lucky. He assured her that they would return to Paris with many times the capital they had acquired from the sale of the land. Charles fancied himself, and probably still does as an ace at Blackjack – if that's the right term.

I don't now know how many days or nights he spent gambling in the casino, but Charles ended up having lost at least half of the forty thousand pounds they had from the sale of Chantal's property. Charles declared that the particular casino or the time he had chosen to place his bets had the shadow of bad luck on it and that they should move on. He persuaded Chantal that he would have better luck in England and when they'd recovered the money he'd lost and trebled his gains, they could have a proper holiday.

Throughout my acquaintance with Sobhraj it was evident that he had no doubts about the notions he concocted or professed to believe. He is certainly calculating but into those calculations enters a streak of reliance on hunches about 'luck' and an unsupportable confidence in his own ability to overcome any circumstance.

The question I asked myself when Chantal told me this story was how much she believed. Did she believe his professions or delusions about 'luck' and his premonitions of hands-down wins in a London casino? I think she did. Her reason never intercepted her infatuation.

\*

If they had been in London longer than that day, had they booked into a hotel? If they had, they weren't returning to it that night. Perhaps they didn't want to pay a pending bill.

No money ever came through. The promises of the repayment of the loan were what came naturally. In no subsequent meeting with either Chantal or Charles, was there any mention of the 600 or so pounds they owed me.

# 11

I had, I thought, enough material to propose both a feature film on the serial crimes of Charles Sobhraj and perhaps a documentary of a particular genre. One of my colleagues at Channel 4, Nicholas Fraser, had become the editor at the BBC of a series called Storyville. This genre of documentary, invented or at least pursued by Nicholas, featured international narratives of some length, each with what one may call a novelistic rather than a journalistic theme and thrust.

I left Channel 4 at the end of 1997 and in the following year, having got Charles's co-operation, I thought that the Charles Sobhraj saga, or what I already knew and could subsequently discover, would make an ideal subject for Storyville.

I called Nicholas and he was, he said very interested and asked me to write up a few pages of a treatment and obtain some permission from Charles and Chantal to feature their lives. The BBC and any broadcaster had to be sure of the legality of their representations of living people. Charles was, unsurprisingly to me, quite willing to have the murders he had perpetrated shown on screen as 'truth' as long as he wasn't associated with having confessed to them. His strategy would be to deny admitting to any murders. His legal co-operation would entail agreeing not to sue the film or the documentary for libel in exchange for as much money as he could bargain for. He would tell the story but when it came on screen or in print he would say it was the film-maker's fantasy.

The film could portray him as a serial killer ---- something he was already internationally known as. It couldn't be used as evidence in any court and he could cry over the damage to his good reputation all the way to the bank.

When I next spoke to Charles and Chantal, I told them about launching the idea with Storyville at the BBC. I merely said that the editor Nicholas Fraser would give it consideration and there was a long way to go to get the narrative, the point of view and several strands of legality right. Nevertheless, I got the distinct impression that Charles and Chantal, unfamiliar with the ways of the TV and film commissioning world and process, thought it a done deal. It wasn't.

The other strand I was examining was, through my Indian journalistic agent and friend Sohrab Irani – 'Soli' to everyone – the possibility of raising Indian or even international production money to make a feature film. Soli was excited by the project and said he'd put out feelers and would come to London and meet Charles and Chantal. He'd leave me to develop the script meanwhile.

I told Charles and Chantal this and again they assumed that the dramatic compulsion of the subject was such that a commission would be forthcoming and the money would pour in. Working in the industry, I entertained no such certainty, especially as, ten years before these efforts and contacts, the Australians had made the TV series on the subject, using Neville and Clarke's book as their source.

With film and TV, one proposes and then one stands and waits.

*

Sorab Irani came from Bombay for a holiday in Europe and stayed with me during the London leg of his tour. He wanted to meet Sobhraj as we'd talked about my acquaintance with him and about Sorab – Soli—raising money for a film about him.

Sobhraj's attitude to a screenplay about him being produced was predictable.

"You can write what you like. You can never say I told you anything. That fellow Richard Neville already did the whole thing in Australia."

"Yes, I saw the serial, it was shown on BBC, Shadow of the Cobra. My mate Art Malik played you."

"He played some character called Charles Sobhraj. Not me," he said.

"So how am I going to write a screenplay if I don't know the facts or have a story? Just make it up?"

"No, no, this phone is not tap, so I can speak. Chantal and I can tell you somethings but I can't say this is some confession. Even the fellow Richard said it was all my confessions but I will continue to say I never signed nothing. You can only call it confession if I speak in front of witnesses and it's all taken down by police or priests or whoever and then I sign it saying it's all true and these are my words. If you can't produce that confession, then you can say you met me and I told you anything! That I killed President Kennedy!"

I understood. The legal rather than the literal meaning of confession was all he cared about. He couldn't be held accountable or prosecuted for what someone else alleged he had said. The distinction was part of Charles's psychological make-up which only a professional is entitled to analyse, diagnose or categorise. Very many times I have been asked by journalists and others whether I think of Sobhraj as a psychopath, a sociopath or other something else. I think such classification is beyond any professional skills I might have. Studies of his behaviour have certainly been made by professionals and they've come to various conclusions, all of them using the two words.

When I was asked what I thought of his mental or moral state I characterised it as being an 'existential amoralist.' If he saw a watch he wanted he would think to himself 'that's a valuable watch – I want it! The problem is it seems to be attached to a human being. If, of course, I get rid of the human being I can have the watch.' The one writer he quoted was Nietzsche. He knew absolutely nothing about Nietzsche's work or philosophy except a few shibboleths such as 'beyond good and evil' and 'morality is in the eye of the beholder' --- not the precise phrases, but words to that effect.

\*

Charles came to London and Sorab (apologies for the closeness of his name to Sobhraj) and I met him on several occasions to discuss the possibilities and finance of the projected film. Chantal's flight from the USA after being confronted by her daughter Usha would, I thought, make a great opening scene.

I worked at the screenplay for the weeks it took and gave it to Soli who had returned to Bombay as he was the prospective producer. Soli said he didn't approve of the script; it wasn't what he had envisaged when he'd agreed to take it on. I am not sure, but I think he approached other writers to fulfil the brief, now that he had Charles's approval to do a film.

I don't know to whom he circulated the screenplay but I relegated it to my unfinished, unpublished and unproduced file of work. But then, a few months later, I received a phone call from Ismael Merchant, the film producer and partner of James Ivory. The Merchant-Ivory brand was in the Oscar winning category of film production. I was a friend of Ismael's and had been on several occasions in talks with him about work and been to his flat for dinner.

"Farrukh, I've just read your screenplay on Sobhraj and think it's fantastic," he said.

"How the hell did you get hold of my script? I haven't sent it out… " I said.

"Oh, come on, you know how this industry works. Someone slipped it to me and I want to discuss it with you. I love it, man."

Wow! That was a welcome surprise! A Merchant-Ivory production?

"Can I meet Sobhraj? Where is he?"

"He's in Paris and he'll certainly come as soon as we call him," I said.

"Yeah, yeah, call him to dinner at my place tomorrow or the next day," Ismael said.

"No, no, no, you don't want to call him to your house," I said.

There was a pause.

"Right, I understand. So, call him to my office in the morning or something."

"No, not even that," I said. "You should meet him on neutral ground."

"What's wrong with the office. He can't do any mischief."

"I think he's given up that sort of mischief," I said, "but what he'll do is charm your secretary or assistants and get their phone numbers and call the office twice a day to ask if you've transferred any money to him and when he can expect a cheque etc. He'll pester your staff."

"Oh OK, I'll book a room and tell you," Ismael said.

Within the hour his secretary called to say they'd provisionally booked a room for the next afternoon in the St James's hotel in Victoria.

I called Charles in Paris and told him that Ismael Merchant was interested in making the film. He said he'd be right over. I told him that the next day would do.

We met in the foyer of the hotel. I thought he'd bring Chantal so was surprised to see Rosanne with him.

Ismael opened the discussion by saying once again that he liked the script and that either he or James Ivory would want to direct it. He turned to Charles and said of course there would be a payment for the rights to the story which his lawyers and agents would assess and make an offer. Charles seemed satisfied with that.

Ismael then asked me what my friend and partner in several enterprises, the renowned film maker Bobby Bedi would expect.

"Why would he expect anything?"

"Isn't he your business partner?" Ismael asked.

"No, we're close friends and have worked together on several things, but he's not a formal partner," I said.

"So, Bobby has nothing to do with this script or project?" Ismael asked

"No, nothing at all," I said.

At this point Charles, who was sitting next to me, put his hand on my thigh and said,

"Fa'ook, I'm very glad to hear that. I hear Bobby Bedi is a dodgy character!"

Ismael and I glanced at each other. It was the moment irony had been the latest victim of the serial killer.

The film was never made by Merchant Ivory. Though Ismael didn't formally contract the script or pay for it, I heard from his subordinates that the firm was in financial trouble and wasn't in any shape to embark even on what wouldn't have been a very expensive film. That's the story of the industry and in a very limited sense, the story of the present scribbler's life in it.

*

That screenplay went nowhere, but some months later another possibility seemed to emerge. My friend Shekhar Kapur, the director of Bandit Queen, a film I wrote and he directed, called me. Shekhar had, after Bandit Queen, made Elizabeth, a film which won an Oscar and had then gone on to make the sequel and other films for Britain and Hollywood. He said he was interested in the Sobhraj story and could I send him three or four pages of a treatment. I spoke to Charles about Shekhar's interest in a film about him and told him I had to write a treatment which Shekhar would show to his producers to raise the finances.

I told him it was the same problem. It had to contain the truth about the crimes he had committed or there would be no point. Charles was sanguine about it.

"You write what you like, Fa'ook, I give you carte blanche!" he said.

I accepted the carte blanche and began my treatment with "There's a killer on the loose! Charles Sobhraj has by some accounts murdered fifty-two people in five countries across Asia……" The synopsis goes on to describe some of the crimes and his modus operandi. The synopsis had, as is required, a beginning, middle and end but not necessarily in that order. I tried to add an element of what the industry calls a 'redemptive theme'.

Shekhar was comfortable with the outline.

"Let's meet Sobhraj. Can you call him? We can meet here at my place," Shekhar said.

He was at the time living in a house in Holland Park.

"I don't think so," I said. "Not a good idea. The weather's good. Let's meet in Holland Park itself. We can say we're in a picnic mood."

I called Sobhraj in Paris and once again he came over. It had been sunny all that August week and the deceptive British weather was not predicted to change. We met at High Street Kensington Underground station. It was again Roseanne who came with him.

We walked to Holland Park. I'd made sandwiches and had a bottle of wine and plastic cups. Shekhar brought a blanket and we settled down for our picnic on the grass under a tree. Shekhar had with him the synopsis of the screenplay. He'd brought it along to ask me for clarifications and perhaps ask Sobhraj some details about incidents or scenes mentioned in it. He was reading it as we squatted on the blanket.

"Is that the film?" Charles asked.

"Yes, the synopsis, a sort of breakdown. Just to get a production company desperately interested," I said.

"Can I see it?" Charles asked. Of course, he would.

"Well, you said you gave me carte blanche and I could write what I thought would get a commission," I said.

"Yes, that's good, but can I see it? I promise I won't say anything," Charles said.

*

Shekhar handed him the stapled sheets. Silence all round. I poured some wine. Charles must have read the first paragraph and skimmed the rest and then he looked up and broke his promise to say nothing.

"Fa'ook, where you get this fifty-two? That's an exaggeration isn't it?"

He said nothing else. I took the synopsis from him and offered him a glass of wine.

So, it was only forty-nine?

Again, as happens in the industry, A-grade-'hot'-director Shekhar got busy with the project that he was already working on and that next Sobhraj screenplay, with its exaggerated premise, never got commissioned or written.

# 12

Several journalists who've called me over the Sobhraj story, or my recollections of my acquaintance with him, ask me where Chantal is. I have no idea and though some of them are diligent investigative types, they haven't been able to trace her whereabouts at all. The internet tells me that she was in constant touch with Charles in Kathmandu jail but was recently told, threateningly, by his new 'wife' the young Nihita Biswas, his Nepalese lawyer's daughter, never to darken its iron bars or closed doors again - and all correspondence between them stopped.

My guess is that tracing her two daughters will give these journalists a lead to Chantal if they need it. The last I heard from her was through a letter she wrote to me which complained, though not at great length, about the way Charles had treated her.

Soon after Chantal had joined Charles in Paris, I had to make a trip to the city for a film I was working on with renowned Pakistani-French director Jamil Dehlavi. Jamil had a one room flat in the Commerce district of Paris and I was staying there. It was a tiny room with an enclosure for a bathroom, a gas ring for a kitchen and its bed four feet in the air in a corner, accessible by a ladder.

Charles rang me and was surprised to hear that I was in Paris. He said he'd come and see me. I gave him the address and he and Chantal turned up that afternoon. After a while, Charles said he was just nipping out for half an hour; he had some work in the arrondissement and Chantal could just stay and talk to me till he returned.

He didn't return. Not in half an hour, one hour or two. Chantal tried his phone but he didn't answer. She was restless. The room was not even big enough to pace in. She would go out into the Rue de Commerce and look for him then come back in case he had returned.

He didn't come back that night and Chantal began, while I fetched dinner and found pillows and duvets for her to sleep on the couch while I climbed to the bed, to try and define the tolerance that she seemed to have for his ways.

I didn't ask the questions, but she started telling me about Charles's birth and childhood as though she was delving into the evolution of his murdering mind. She told me – and Charles would bring up bits of this chronology in chats and discussions through the years – that Charles's father was a Sindhi businessman, probably dealing in gems and jewellery in South East Asia in the early 1940s. India had not achieved independence from British rule in those years and Sindh was still part of undivided India, though after 1947 it was part of Pakistan. The Hindu Sindhis, who had not earlier migrated to other parts of India, now sought refuge from Muslim-led pogroms in the truncated India and arrived as refugees when their state had been allocated as a whole by the British Raj to the new state of Pakistan.

Sobhraj Bhavnani's family, or at least part of it, had migrated before Partition to Bombay and Poona in Western India. It was there, when I was at college, that I was acquainted with Raj Advani, Sobhraj Bhavnani's sister's son and Charles's first cousin.

Sobhraj Bhavnani is constantly referred to in the book By Neville and Clarke as 'Hotchand' but, as I said before, neither Chantal nor Charles ever used that name for him in my presence. Charles's mother was a Vietnamese lady who formed a relationship with Sobhraj Bhavnani on his business sojourns in Saigon and in 1944 she gave birth to the boy they called Gurumukh Bhavnani. I have known Charles to say that his name was Gurudev rather than

Gurumukh, but I may have misheard this particular pronouncement.

Bhavnani went back to India and the relationship was unviable, though he never disowned his son Gurumukh. Charles' mother subsequently married a French soldier who was on duty in what was then the French colony of Vietnam. The world was in turmoil in the early 1940s with the Second World War in Europe and the invasion of China, Singapore and Burma by the Japanese Axis forces. In 1945, when the war ended with the surrender of Germany and Japan, Ho chi Min and the VietMinh communist forces launched their insurrection against French colonialism in the villages and cities of Vietnam. The French forces fought a losing battle against the guerrilla tactics of the VietMinh, later to be transformed when the French withdrew and the USA sent its armed forces to 'battle communism', into the VietCong.

The French soldier who had married Gurumukh Bhavnani's mother, didn't want a child whom he had virtually adopted, called by an Indian name. He renamed him Charles after his hero, the liberator of France, Charles De Gaulle, and decided that his surname would be his birth-father's first name, Sobhraj to distinguish him from his own children. Hence Gurumukh Bhavnani becomes Charles Sobhraj.

Chantal wanted to convince me that Charles's moral, immoral or amoral stance as I thought of it, was attributable to the traumas of his childhood. A child whose adoptive father changed his name may have been a factor. Chantal never related to me what she knew of his relationship with his mother and her husband after the French army withdrew from Vietnam and the family moved to Paris.

The dramatic part of her story was that Charles as a young child of four, five or six lived in war-torn Saigon and often stepped over dead bodies lying bleeding, maimed and completely disfigured by bombs, grenades and bullets or even rotting in the streets. That experience, she was certain, may not excuse an indifference to death but might go some way towards explaining it.

It may have been that night, when I fell intermittently asleep in the raised bunk bed and heard Chantal staying watchfully awake and restlessly shifting around all night in anticipation of Charles's return, that she told me a bit about his life and crimes in Paris. All I recall is that he was convicted for stealing cars and then for forgery. She also alluded to one incident in which Charles robbed a household at gunpoint.

It was to avoid arrest on one of these charges that they decided, after they were married, to escape from France. She said he never felt he fitted in there. Though he was close to his step-siblings, he didn't feel very French at all. He was a person of the East and would seek his fortune in it.

By that morning in Paris, Charles had still not returned. I made Chantal coffee and she left. Neither she nor Charles contacted me again while I was in Paris.

# 13

Chantal came several times with Charles to London. On one occasion, crossing the Channel in his cream- coloured, rickety old Mercedes by ferry he drove into London and called me.

Margaret Peacock and I met them in town and Chares drove us through Soho with Margaret who gets car-sick in the back seats of vehicles sitting next to him in front.

Charles is a careless driver and in a crowded street, driving through Soho ignored several pedestrians who, by right, were walking across a pedestrian crossing. Charles didn't stop the car but drove straight across the marked black and white crossing, causing several of the walkers to fall back to save themselves being run over. It all happened in a flash and Margaret grabbed Charles's wrist as he held the steering wheel and shouted

"Stop! You could have killed someone!"

Charles glanced sideways at her through slit eyes. She realised what the impact of her outburst was on him and Chantal! No more was said. Charles drove on.

*

Chantal, quite devoted to Charles confided in Margaret.

"We are going to get married again," she said, "and I know Charles wants Farrukh to be his best man. But don't say anything until Charles asks him."

Charles never asked me.

# 14

Two days after Christmas on the 27th Dec 1999 Charles phoned me from Paris.

"You know this thing, the hi-jack in Kandahar, Fa'ook?"

I said I did. It was international news. An Indian Airlines flight IC814 had taken off from Kathmandu in Nepal with

176 people on board. It was headed to Indira Gandhi international Airport in Delhi. After it took off, five of the passengers who were members of the Harkat-ul-Mujaheddin terror outfit of Pakistan, supported by the Pakistani army's ISI, hijacked the plane using weapons and explosives they had smuggled on board to threaten the crew and passengers.

It was a serious hi-jack to which the pilot and crew succumbed and the plane was forced to land at first in Amritsar. After two other stops, it was refuelled at a United Arab Republic airport and then ordered to land in Kandahar in Afghanistan.

The terrorists threatened to kill all the passengers if their demands to free five notorious and convicted terrorists, captive in Indian jails, were not set free. One of these was Masood Azhar. The news of the hi-jack and the hi-jackers' demands was national news.

"What about it?" I asked Sobhraj.

"Listen, I know Masood Azhar and can talk to him. He is my friend. He is in charge of the whole thing and I can get him to free the hostages," Charles said.

"Masood is the fellow who was with you in Tihar jail?" I asked.

"He is still there and I know he is leading these hi-jackers. They are demanding his release."

"And four other terrorists," I said.

"You must be knowing people in the Indian government. I can talk to Masood and get the hostages freed alive."

I was aware that Charles had cultivated a friendship with Masood in Tihar jail, even though he had, unbeknown to Masood, betrayed him. Perhaps he could negotiate some sort of deal. I didn't know anyone in the Indian government. But it occurred to me that I did know and was really good friends with some very senior journalists, the editors of the Times of India for instance, Dilip Padgaonkar in Delhi and Darryl D'Monte in Bombay. I could call them and they would certainly have a hot line to government ministers and probably to the office of the PM Atal Behari Vajpayee who would be dealing personally with this crisis. Then the name of Ashok Jaitley, a friend and now a senior civil servant in Delhi flashed through my mind. Perhaps he'd be the better bet. I called Ashok. He answered.

I told him that I was acquainted with Sobhraj and asked him if he knew who that was. Of course he did. I said Sobhraj was a personal friend of Masood Azhar who was undoubtedly in charge of this hi-jack operation. Sobhraj was offering to negotiate on behalf of the Indian government to get the hostages in the plane on the tarmac in Kandahar airport released. I said I didn't know what deal Sobhraj would or could cut with Masood, but was confident that whatever it was, it could work.

Ashok said this was certainly an avenue to explore. The country and the entire government didn't want this hostage crisis to end badly. There were, he said, recriminations about the lapse of security on the Indian Airlines desk, at the gates etc. which had allowed five terrorists and their weapons on board. And there were going to be repercussion against Nepal for the lack of security at Kathmandu airport, but that would all be dealt with in the future. The immediate task, he agreed, was to get the hostages out alive and he would get to Jaswant Singh, the Foreign Minister, personally and get back to me and thence to Sobhraj.

I said I'd wait for his answer and if it were done when 'tis done, then 'twere well it were done quickly.

I called Charles and told him I had spoken to a member of the Indian government who was going to put the plan to the Foreign Minister entrusted with getting the hostages home alive, and call me back.

Ashok called me back five or six hours later. He said he'd had extensive discussions with Jaswant about the offer from Sobhraj. They had discussed it with several members or possibly the head of RAW, the Indian CIA and even military personnel. Jaswant had said that tempting though it was as a short cut to negotiations with the hostages, he didn't want the Indian or the world's media reporting that the Indian government had used the offices of a serial killer to do a deal with Pakistani terrorists. So, no they could but wouldn't use that avenue.

I had to convey the decision to Charles. The Indian government would go it without his help.

"Masood won't agree with them," he said. "He hates them."

Five days after the siege began, Jaswant, having flown to Kandahar and negotiated with the hi-jackers on the tarmac, agreed to release the five prisoners from Indian jails in exchange for a return of the aircraft and all its passengers and crew. It was seen as a climbdown and shabby deal on the part of the Indian government, but at least the hostages, all but one unfortunate passenger who had been killed by the hi-jackers to prove their deadly intent and resolve at the beginning of the saga at Kandahar, were released alive.

Masood Azhar was released and sent back to Pakistan where he received a hero's welcome. He went on to lead one of the most ruthless outfits of Pakistani terror called Jaish-e-Mohammed. He remained firm friends with Charles who visited him in Pakistan.

*

In interviews with the British media from Kathmandu jail, Sobhraj claimed to have been instrumental in getting the hostages on flight IC814 released. If he was, it wasn't through the abortive contact which I made for him through Ashok Jaitley. Or was it? Yes, I had given Ashok Sobhraj's phone number.

# 15

After 9/11 and President George Bush's American invasion of Afghanistan to track down Osama Bin Laden and suppress the Islamicist Taliban, Charles told me he was going to that country on a humanist mission. He said he had been invited to survey the state of orphans who lived in camps as a result of the Afghan conflict and see what could be done to redeem their lives.

It was the sort of mission that some UNICEF ambassadorial official could have spoken about. Did Charles really believe that he was now some sort of Mother Teresa or was this a fabricated cover for some more sinister motive? I have always found it difficult to decide whether the fantasist within Charles sometimes gets the better of the conniving, criminal strategist. Maybe he does sometimes get carried away and actually believe the story he has concocted.

On this occasion it occurred to me that it could quite easily be true. Charles could well be going to the orphanages of Afghanistan in order to offer them money or other material assistance as an emissary of Masood Azhar who was now leading the Islamicist terror outfit Jaish-e-Muhammad. These gangs must see themselves as the patrons of orphans whose parents had been killed in the Islamicist or Talibanic cause in Afghanistan. It was after all, the Pakistani state, in the form of the Inter-Services Intelligence (ISI), the state within a state of Pakistan, which had organised the Taliban and set them against the Americans who were Pakistan's international patrons and allies, supplying them with military assistance and subsistence of all sorts. Wheels within wheels?

Charles never told me in any detail about what he was doing with Masood or who exactly he had met through him. What he did say was that he would receive the protection of Pakistan's fundamentalist groups not only in that country but wherever he travelled. I knew he had travelled to Afghanistan after meeting Masood on its borders somewhere. I was soon to find out why.

*

My phone rang, again in the early hours of a morning and Charles said he had to see me urgently.

"I am in England in a hotel on the M25 motorway. Can you come over, it will be very profitable for you," he said.

"I don't know what you mean. It's six in the morning, Charles. And I am not after any profit."

"It's a surprise. I will tell you everything, Fa'ook, just come and have breakfast here."

I was wide awake and I admit, curious. How would turning up at some motel on the M25 be helpful to me in any way? I even wondered if he had decided to confess to his crimes.

I got the details of the location from him. When he gave them to me, I recognised them as a pub off the motorway, a mock-Tudor building, which I must have driven past a hundred times. I'd never stopped there but knew the name.

The peripheral motorway was getting heavy with traffic at seven in the morning as I drove there, but I got there and parked in the car park. Charles was waiting for me in the foyer of the pub which had rooms to let. He said he was glad to see me and led me back to the car park, calling his associates on the phone as he did.

We walked towards a large van parked in a corner and were joined by two guys whom he had summoned. One must have been in his forties and the other in his twenties. They were clearly continentals and were wearing thick black leather jackets. They could have been extras in a French crime TV series. Charles introduced us and the young man used a key to open the back doors of the van. They invited me to look in.

The van was packed with what looked like old furniture: sets of chairs stacked together, ornate chests and small tables neatly packed together and taking up most of the square inches the interior offered.

"What's this about?" I turned to Charles.

"Antiques, ole man, French and Belgian antiques. We want to set up a business."

I must have looked puzzled.

"We need you as a partner," Charles said.

I was more than puzzled.

"I don't know anything about antiques," I said.

"That's all right, my friends know all about getting them and everything. What we need is someone who can get a lease on a shop-front or building. We can't do it. I am French and these boys are Belgian. We need someone with a British passport and a British bank account. And that's you. It's easy if you sign for the lease. The business will pay mortgage, everything."

"If you want to open an antique shop, it should be in Portobello Road or Camden Town or somewhere people go to buy antiques," I said. "I've already got my name on a mortgage and I doubt if any bank or company will let me extend to another lease."

"Our money can fix all that," Charles said. "And listen man, we are willing to pay you as a partner - £100,000."

He looked in my face to see how the mention of that sum had hit me.

"Just to get a lease on a shop?"

"It could be anywhere, man, any street. A London address, that's all."

Then he motioned to the Belgians to lock the van and said, "Come with me upstairs?"

"Breakfast upstairs?"

"No, no man, first I want to show you something."

I followed Charles to the room he had booked the night before. He opened one of the drawers of the chest and took out a pack of what looked like brochures. He handed two of them to me.

"Have a look, sit down," Charles said and shut the room door behind me.

I sat on the bed and looked at the brochures he'd handed me. The covers had Cyrillic script. Inside were photographs of various models of weapons: automatic guns, large-mouthed cannons which I assumed were mortars, anti-aircraft artillery and even armoured cars. The captions to the photographs and the writing in the catalogues were, I assumed, in Russian.

Sobhraj was standing against the chest of drawers staring at me intently but coolly to gauge my reaction. I looked up at him and then opened the second brochure. It was also full of photographs and paragraphs in Russian.

This second brochure, apart from what looked to me like Sten and Bren guns and grenades of different sizes, even contained pictures of boats, presumably military ones. All deadly weapons, great and small.

"Why am I looking at these?" I looked up and asked.

"The antique is a front," Charles said, very casually. "We are really selling these armaments to groups all over the world. You won't be involved in any of that. We have people working on that front."

"Getting arms from Russia and selling them to whom?"

"We are actually based in San Marino which is like a free port and there is not much tax and checking, but we need a front in London for banking and everything. That's where you come in. I told you there's a hundred thousand we can give you very soon."

"Why would Russia sell you weapons to sell, if they can flog them to foreign governments?"

"This is not the billion-dollar new weapons trade, ole man. These are from dumps. Not Russia. We get all this in the catalogues from all those states which were in the Soviet Union and are now independent places, like Belarus and Azerbaijan and other places where Russia has dumped all these weapons which are for them out of date. These countries sell them to us, because they also want to move on with their arms etc. These are one model too early but very useful to certain groups."

"What groups?"

Sobhraj smiled.

"I heard you were a Marxist and revolutionary, Fa'ook," he said. "So we are selling to people who are fighting revolutions and need the armaments."

"You mean terrorist groups?"

"I don't know what you want to call them. But what's the difference between what Americans did in Vietnam or what our customers are doing for liberation. War is like that and whether we are selling or buying or whatever, the world will go on as it is. You know that."

It was my turn to smile.

"You seriously want me to get involved in some illegal armaments trade?"

"Getting a lease on a shop is not illegal. That's all."

"Charles, there is no way I can convince any mortgage lender on my occasional writer's income to give me a second mortgage. "

"You must say -- if you can't get a lease we can find the whole money to buy a place outright."

"Yeah, and send me to jail for tax-avoidance? You think the Inland Revenue or the police will believe that I suddenly got hold of enough money to buy a building? "

He didn't hesitate.

"We can set up a film company and say we bought some film screenplay from you for half a million pounds," he said. "Then you buy the building with that and we could make a side deal." He was serious.

"Charles you just said I was a revolutionary and revolutionaries shouldn't do crooked deals to buy buildings. There's no way, even practically, even I was tempted to get involved, which I am not, that I can pull this off. If I did a deal for half a million pounds for a screenplay, my literary agent would sue me. So please count me out, ole man – as you would say."

He said "OK. I have to think of someone else but you were my best man. I thought of you first."

I breathed a sigh of relief as I drove onto the motorway. I was thinking of the old mafia adage about making someone an offer they couldn't refuse.

But as I drove, I thought of our visit to John and Charles and what Chantal had told me about him betraying his contacts to America in exchange for a new life for them. The Masood incident, of handing over Masood's telephone contacts to RAW also came to mind.

Was he really dealing with groups like the Taliban? His partners were obviously up to their necks in this business, but was he stringing them along? I was picturing his expressionless face as he showed me the catalogues - his raised cheekbones and slightly slanting eyes with a shock of thick purple-black hair which inevitably came from his cross of Indo-Vietnamese genes.

I thought I wanted to never have known the man, never to have got involved, even peripherally with his dealings. The reason I had driven him to Grantchester was at first just a favour to keep his acquaintance and then curiosity about the intrigue to which it might lead.

Did I believe Chantal when she told me that Charles was strengthening his contacts with terrorists and arms and drug networks in order to betray them? What was that about? And was this trip part of that strategy? Did it seem a way of getting back to respectability, of decisively changing sides and finally being instrumentally on the side of the law?

*

While reading Solzhenitsyn, the accounts of the Gulags, or while reading holocaust literature, we undoubtedly say to ourselves 'never again'. But historical cruelty is relentless and humans won't give it up. Yesterday it was Hitler and the Nazis. In our time it's the religious fanatics who distort religion into death cults. Mass murder in the name of religious purity. If humans were ever to be subjected to such systematic torture and extermination, if they were ever again to lose the status of humans, it would be by the acts and under the governance of the 'pure', of the Taliban, of the Wahabis, of the holy who seek unfettered power.

I believed that he was selling arms to the Taliban and perhaps had plans to betray them too. And if Charles's betrayal went ahead and if it worked, that in itself would bring large forces into play. I was asking myself what I would have done if, knowing what we do today, I had had the chance to blow Hitler's cover in his Munich days or to have Stalin, Koba the butcher, assassinated in 1917.

I didn't know to whom or under what deal CS would make his betrayal but it would have to be such as to lead to cutting one of the veins of fanaticism and terror in our world. In the end would Sobhraj's betrayal of terrorists and death-cultists be seen in balance against his own series of murders? His intention was to emerge as a hero, an accomplice and inside-operative of the forces of law and order – if a disreputable organisation such as the CIA, with its record of double dealings and criminal activity can be labelled such.

I ask myself today why didn't I go to the authorities and tell them I was aware of a plot to sell armaments or to launder money? The answer is I didn't know whom to tell. I couldn't very well go to my local police station and tell them where I'd been and what I'd seen. They would probably have me carried away in a strait-jacket. And then there was the possibility that Charles was really playing a double game and intended to hand over his terrorist customers, and even his associates who sold arms to them, to the CIA? Any complaint by myself would stymie such an international plan and allow the terrorist organisations who were supposedly buying arms to perpetrate their wickedness.

Charles's plan of setting up an antique front didn't materialise, at least not in London. Perhaps this gang opened an antique shop in Paris or Amsterdam. I heard nothing more about a shop, but I did hear about further and even more dangerous or consequential arms dealing.

\*

All of Charles's proposals to me weren't criminal. He approached me once saying he was giving up other dealings to go into the wine trade. He said that France and Spain dumped a lot of surplus, perfectly-drinkable wine and he could buy barrels of it at negligible prices. Could I find a bottling plant, so we could import the wine into the UK, add the UK government's tax on alcohol and still sell the wine at extremely competitive prices?

I had no inclination to go into any wine business, but found his calculations fascinating. With a partner capable of administering the plan, perhaps Charles could have become a serial vintner.

But he was someone who moved on. He didn't mention the wine proposal again.

# 16

It wasn't long before Charles rang again from Paris. This was early 2002.

"Fa'ook, what is Wed Mercuwy?"

Having a Natural Sciences – physics – degree from Cambridge, though never practising in the scientific trades, I keep up, out of interest, with developments in physics that I can understand. I don't know if I ever confided this qualification or interest to Charles, but he seemed to ask the question as though he was sure that I'd know the answer.

As it happened, I did. I had just written a screenplay with that very title. The story of the film which was subsequently produced and screened and went to various festivals, was a terrorist attack by young British-Asian men who were forced to seek refuge in a restaurant and hold hostages against their capture by the security forces and police. I could answer him.

"It's something the Russians claim to have discovered and fabricated. It's supposedly an unstable product of antimony which can be used as a nuclear trigger. It's used, the Russians claim, to set off an atomic bomb – much more effective and compact than the explosives used so far. But, very many scientists around the world doubt if it exists. They think it's a Soviet bluff. That being said even American scientists say that Red Mercury may well exist but is unstable."

"Is it dangerous to handle?"

"I have no idea. I suppose the Russian scientists made it safe for the Russian military or rocket-wallahs who handle warheads to use. Why?" I asked.

"I'll tell you after," he said.

That exchange intrigued me for a few minutes. Perhaps Charles was reading some book or articles about nuclear sciences. I forgot the phone call. But I recalled it later when, enquiring after Charles's whereabouts and his availability to speak to Nick, the editor of Storyville at the BBC who was still trying to decide whether his story was worth telling and whether he'd co-operate and sign release forms, Chantal said he had gone to Bahrain.

"What's he doing in Bahrain?"

"You know his business. I don't want to say anything on the phone, but he's meeting some customers. Selling jewellery, I think."

Back to that, I thought. I hope he doesn't kill his customers to retrieve the gems – but I didn't say it. I forgot the conversation. There were things to do. I didn't link Charles's enquiry about red mercury to his trip to Bahrain. I should have.

*

Britain was soon convulsed in controversy about Tony Blair's decision to ally with George Bush's determination to invade Iraq and topple the regime of Saddam Hussein. Blair's declaration in parliament and to the nation was that Iraq had weapons of mass destruction or WMD as they came to be known. These were supposed to be chemical, biological and nuclear weapons which Saddam's regime had developed and stockpiled in order to threaten the region and possibly Britain's outposts. Blair's publicist Alasdair Campbell told the press that these weapons could be deployed against the UK's military bases in Cyprus in a matter of 45 minutes.

Blair and Campbell said they based their pronouncements, and hence the decision to get parliament to ratify entering a war against Iraq, on a report from secret services which confirmed Saddam's acquisition and stockpiling of these WMD. The report published in September 2002 by Campbell was the central justification for committing Britain to the war alliance with the USA. The report was, even at the time, challenged and was eventually labelled the 'dodgy dossier'.

Controversy raged over the decision to risk British soldiers' lives in this conflict in the volatile Middle East. There were demonstrations and marches against the war-mongering Blair. Did he imagine that this act was his 'Falklands Moment' which would, through a show of unflinching British strength against a dictatorial regime, win him unprecedented popularity with a historical dimension? Many believed he was just kowtowing to Bush and the USA in order to strengthen the 'special alliance' between the English-speaking countries. We doubted whether he and his more-than-spokesman Campbell believed that Saddam's dictatorship was a real threat to Britain.

The rest of the European Union countries declined to join the war but news of civilian casualties from the US and UK bombings of Baghdad and other cities began to be published. Saddam's regime seemed doomed. There was footage on UK TV of enraged Iraqi citizens pulling down the statue of Saddam Hussein and then the news that the dictator had gone into hiding as the allied troops defeated his armies and took cursory military control of the country.

In my columns for Indian newspapers I had expressed the opinion that there was no doubt that Saddam was a dictatorial ruler who had deployed the most horrific campaign against any revolt from sections of his own population, but he was, in the turbulent Middle East, a cat who kept several nasty fundamentalist rats at bay. In Middle Eastern terms, he could be seen as a modernizing force.

My columns were of course speculative and written from a journalistic distance. I even argued that the US and UK could have negotiated an economic and educational deal with Saddam. They could have bargained with him, offered him thousands of places in western universities to train his professional classes. They could have given him aid in exchange for oil. He could have made gestures towards democracy and even perhaps made some peace treaty with Israel. With declining revenue from oil, Saddam might have agreed to talks on such lines.

It was a cry in the wilderness. Bush and Blair's war cost hundreds of thousands of lives. It was, in my view and that of millions of Britons and Americans, an unjustified war. Or was it? I kick myself for not connecting Sobhraj's phone call about Red Mercury to any of this.

## 17

In 2001 I wrote a biography of the Trinidadian Marxist philosopher and cricket commentator CLR James. A journalist called Peter Oborne, a cricket enthusiast, wrote a very kind review of it in The Spectator. Defying writer-reviewer protocol I wrote him a two-word thank you on e-mail and he replied subsequently with a request for any information I might have on CLR's attitude towards South African cricket and the politics and boycotts that bedeviled the all-white team. He was interested in CLR's view of or contact with Basil D'Oliviera. I might have given him a few sentences from memory, but at the time I thought I didn't want any further contact with an overly right-wing weekly such as The Spectator.

Later, that further contact came in very useful, and yes, Sobhraj was involved. This is an account of it.

The huge question at the time was whether the Weapons of Mass Destruction which had taken the country into war actually existed. Dissent and controversy raged in the media and elsewhere. The dodgy dossier was challenged as reports from the war front seemed to say that there was no evidence of manufactories of chemical or biological warfare and the US and UK's victorious troops had found nothing that represented a depot, a depository or launching site for missiles to deliver nuclear warheads.

There was the Blair contention that Saddam's regime and armed forces had destroyed every site which could be identified as a place where, missiles, nuclear warheads, nuclear bombs or anything of the kind were manufactured or stored or kept ready to be activated. But nothing was found and such a job of erasure would have been formidable and would almost certainly have left traces.

Opinion on the left in Britain, including myself, regretted the loss of life, the devastation and the release of predictably nasty forces in the Middle East. There was no triumphalism on our part following the disclosure by the US and UK armies that no WMD had been found in Iraq. Blair was in trouble. He and his spokesman Alistair Campbell would have some explaining to do as they would be held to account about their interpretation of the dossier.

And then the thought of that phone conversation with Charles recurred. The talk about Bahrain, business, Belarus, Kazakhstan, San Marino, the inn hotel on the M25, the catalogues he showed me in his first floor room, the antiques in the truck, the two Belgians, the London shop front proposal, £100,000….. and yes, red mercury. Red – fucking—mercury – a nuclear trigger!

I called Charles.

"Now give me a straight answer, why did you ask me about red mercury?"

"I wanted to know what it was."

"Stop fooling around. That's obvious, but why did you want to know what it was and why did you go to Bahrain?"

"How you know about Bahrain Fa'ook?"

"Doesn't matter, tell me why you went to Bahrain and whether red mercury had anything to do with it!"

"You know about my business with my partners and where we get the stuff."

"Yes, I do," I said.

"There was an enquiry from some customers about red mercury and they said if we could get some, we should go to Bahrain to seal the deal."

"So you went to do the deal. Did you have the red mercury with you? Who were these customers?"

"We were offered the supply of red mercury and these Arab fellows wanted to buy it and were enquiring about it. I have all the evidence, man. I have recordings of the meeting and e-mails in code about the same things."

I took a deep breath.

"Who were these customers you met in Bahrain?"

"Why you want to know, Fa'ook? They were Arabs."

"Arabs? Could they have been Iraqis?"

"Of course, Fa'ook. They must have been. They were very well dressed in Western suits," Charles said.

"And you have recordings of their conversations and e-mails about meeting them? Is red mercury mentioned in any of these?"

"Of course, sometimes in code because they and we didn't want to put such things down in e-mails, but the code is there and clear."

"I don't think you realise what you're telling me," I said.

"How you mean?" he asked.

"You are perhaps sitting on one of the biggest news stories in the world. I hate it, but the truth is the truth," I said.

For all his reputation of international cunning and savvy, I couldn't understand that he hadn't made the connection.

"What truth?" Charles asked.

"That if Iraqis were enquiring about red mercury, a trigger for nuclear weapons, then Saddam Hussein might well have been in possession of or planning to be in possession of Weapons of Mass Destruction. In other words, Bush and Blair and the dossier that Blair and Campbell used as reasons for the UK going to war were right. Or possibly right."

Silence.

"Can you come over to London, right away?"

"I am coming now," he said.

"Bring your e-mails and recordings of the meeting and stuff with you," I said. "And keep your mobile on, even on the Eurostar or however you are coming and I'll tell you when and where I can fix contacts in the British press. This is a huge scoop and you can make your own calculations and bargains."

"I'm coming now," he said.

I put the phone down and looked in my phone's addresses for Peter Oborne's number. I thought he had phoned me once and I had recorded it. The Spectator was and is a blatantly right-wing magazine, and even though they may have had an aversion to Tony Blair, it was quite likely that they were in favour of the war and perhaps would welcome some proof of its having been a justified one. I called him and told him why I was calling. I said Sobhraj would be in London that evening. He said it sounded like a huge scoop and he'd speak to Boris Johnson, the then editor of the Spectator and get back to me.

In a few minutes he called back to say I should bring Sobhraj to his house at 7.30 in the morning and Boris would be there too. He gave me the address in Highbury.

I called Sobhraj who said he'd catch the train at the Gare du Nord that night and we arranged to meet at around 7 the next morning at Highbury and Islington station. He said he would arrive that evening and book a room in the usual lodging house he used in Victoria for the night.

We went to Oborne's house at the appointed time and Boris Johnson turned up on his bicycle. Mrs Oborne gave us coffee and breakfast snacks and Charles related his story to Boris and Peter. He said he had proof in the form of e-mails and recordings of everything he was saying. He didn't offer to produce them there and then. Boris listened very attentively.

"It's too big a story for The Spectator," he said. "It should break in a broadsheet. I can call Mike at the Daily Telegraph."

He must have mentioned Mike's full name but I can't recall it. The Telegraph is another rag of right-wing opinion which I wouldn't read. Mike must have been at the time its military or war correspondent, or perhaps just a senior writer.

I said I had things to do and would leave Sobhraj to get in touch with Mike when he arrived. I left the gathering and went my way. That evening I got a call from Mike who introduced himself and said, "Your man Sobhraj is asking for a few hundred thousand pounds just to show us proof that he has this story. Then he says he will give us the details. We are not permitted to pay for our news stories – that's against the law," he said.

I could sense from what he was saying that he wanted me to persuade Charles to provide the evidence of the story he had or for me to do the same if I had access to the proof.

"I am afraid I have nothing to do with this story," I said. "I did introduce Sobhraj to Boris Johnson, but that's the end of it for me. I am not part of it and don't know what evidence Charles has, but I can confirm that he enquired about red mercury from me, before the war started. I also know that he has something to do with arms procurement, getting armaments from ex-Soviet countries who have stocks of old Russian arms and perhaps refurbishing them or something. I can tell you for certain that he went to Bahrain to do some business. I am sure there are others who can testify to all that. I know that he uses all sorts of forged and stolen passports to travel sometimes so I don't know if he entered Bahrain as Charles Sobhraj or as Adolf Raskolnikov. I know he'll bargain so I'll leave you to it. Sorry I can't help further."

He understood.

A few hours later Charles called.

"This fellow is offering me fifteen thousand pounds for this story, ole man. That's peanuts. I can sell it to America for a proper price," Charles said. "I got some contacts."

I supposed then that he meant the CIA contacts he had obtained through John Ranelagh's introduction.

"I can try and get hold of other contacts," I said. "I know people who work for The Guardian and The Times. I could try them tomorrow, if you want. You can talk to them. They may be willing to meet your demands."

"I can't wait man. I have to get to Paris tonight because I have a flight early tomorrow. Where are you Fa'ook?"

I said I'd just been at a studio across Lambeth Bridge, doing an interview for Indian TV.

"Is that close to Victoria?" he asked.

"Not far, why?"

"I want to speak to you, but not on the phone. If you have half an hour before I get going, can we meet in Victoria at my hotel or somewhere near here? Its urgent."

It was a few minutes' drive. I didn't know what the urgency was. Did he want to hand over the evidence of his red mercury sale to me? I said I'd meet him at a pub called The Shakespeare near Victoria station and we could talk there or meet there and move on.

# 18

It was then that he told me, for reasons I have never understood, about where he was going and why. It was a brief talk as he had packed his overnight bag and was heading for Paris. The next morning, he said he was leaving for Nepal, for Kathmandu via Pakistan.

I was, from the books and articles about him, aware that he is reported to have killed two people in Kathmandu. This must have been in late 1976 or early 1977, after his escape from Thailand and before he poisoned the French tourists and was caught and jailed for it. In Kathmandu, in his guise of a gem merchant, he is supposed to have beguiled a young American hippy called Connie Jo Bronzish and her Canadian boyfriend Laurent Carriere and stabbed and burnt their bodies which were beyond recognition and discovered in different outlying areas of Kathmandu.

I didn't want to say 'but you've murdered people there' but I did say:

"Isn't it unsafe for you?"

"Why you say that Fa'ook. I am as safe as I want to be. I might go with a different passport."

"What's so urgent in Kathmandu? You have this story under your belt. That could make reasonable money for you. As you say, you've got evidence which you can sell to a US newspaper and I'm sure they are more lax about paying for leads and leaks and complete world-shattering scoops like this one."

"That's right, but I can deal with that when I get to the US."

"You plan to go to the USA?"

He didn't answer that but kept a straight face.

"You know my business and you know that I am friends with Masood?"

"I know," I said. "So?"

"He is very close with the Taliban in Afghanistan. He is connecting me. They will come and we can meet in Kathmandu, a neutral place for plenty reasons. Pakistan is not safe for them because it's divided. Some want to support the Taliban and some want to eliminate them. That's Pakistan. I can go there any time because the military who work with Masood will give me top protection."

"So why do you want to meet the Taliban?" I asked, though I thought I knew the answer. He was selling them armaments.

"Listen Fa'ook, the Taliban don't have anything except heroin which they sell in Pakistan and then they smuggle it to India and some they can sell in Tajikstan and these rubbish places. All they get is Pakistani and Indian rupees and some rouble kind of money. Me and my partners, we don't need rupees and junk money. We want dollars and pounds and Euros for the weapons that they want."

"I could have guessed," I said.

"But they have no contacts and nothing in Europe and America where the real market for heroin is. I am getting my Chinese Triad friends from Paris to come to Kathmandu and set up a deal and a trail for the heroin which can pass through Pakistan to the Triads who have a network of drug sales all over the world – every European country and America and even Australia. That will get in the real money and with that the Taliban can buy weapons from me. They want everything you saw in those catalogues I showed you, remember?"

I remembered. It would be a three-way deal. Heroin from the Taliban who control the countryside, sold by the Triads who then hand the money to Charles to ship weapons to the Taliban.

"That's elaborate and evil," I said.

His expression, normally dead pan or betraying the pride he took in his deviousness, now for the first time in our acquaintance, looked sad. He nodded.

"It will all be over quickly, and I will leave it then to the CIA and Americans. And that's the end of all this. I can start again in the US; do straight business," he said.

"So why are you telling me all this?"

"Because you think I am a serial killer and arms dealer and am on the side of people like the Taliban who want to convert everyone to be Muslim."

I didn't know what to say to that apart from 'yes, it is what I think, because it's true. That is what you are and that is whom you support with your red mercury and catalogue of weaponry for terror.' I didn't say it. Instead I asked:

"Why tell me your plans?"

"Because that's not all my plans. You know you introduced me to that fellow who wrote the history of the CIA? I got in touch with them and made a deal. I told them who I am meeting in Kathmandu and they will then have information on the Triad drug network in America and solid information on the Taliban."

"You're going to double-cross them?"

I couldn't believe it.

"This is why I told you. See? I can finish with arms-dealing and dodgy people and go and live in the US and have a new life and then you can come and visit me there," he said, breaking into a smile.

"Isn't it dangerous?" I asked, "This double game?"

"Fa'ook, when have I run away from 'dangerous'?"

He looked at his watch. It was time to go, he said. He was taking the underground to St Pancras.

"I will call you from an American mobile number," he said as he left.

I went back to my car. A new leaf? What would the CIA do? Get contacts, names, locations and information about the Triads and Taliban and their weapons and drug networks and close in on them when they thought it strategically advantageous or necessary?

That he was reputed to have murdered two people twenty-eight years previously didn't seem to have entered his calculations. Or perhaps it had and he was confident that there could be no evidence that anyone could bring against him. It was before DNA tests entered forensics.

## 19

According to the reports of his arrest and trial in Kathmandu, instead of staying the couple of days he had told me were needed to do the deal with the Triads and the Taliban representatives and hand the information and perhaps the people over to the CIA, he had actually stayed in the city for two weeks.

The reports said he was travelling on a French passport with an assumed identity and had spent his evenings in a basement casino playing blackjack. He had been spotted by a journalist who had been on his tail twenty-eight years ago. The journalist, the reports said, identified him and alerted the police. A police officer who had interrogated Sobhraj after the body of Connie Jo Bronzich had been discovered was called into service and Charles was arrested in the casino and charged with her murder.

By all accounts, the records of the murder were either sparse or didn't exist. The convictions that Charles faced, first for the murder of Connie Jo and then, years later when he was already serving a life sentence, for the second murder of Laurent Carriere, were by any standards of evidence in a Western court, unsafe. But the Nepalese courts, in convicting Sobhraj for these murders, accepted the word of the policemen who had investigated the murders twenty-eight years previously. One of these policemen had interrogated Charles who was all those years ago after the murders, attempting to leave Nepal and presented himself to them as a Dutch citizen tourist. He wasn't arrested at the time as they hadn't any concrete proof of his guilt --- at least not till after he had left the country.

So where did Charles's plans go wrong? Why isn't he enjoying a life in America as Don Juan III or whoever with a CIA-provided ranch in Cactus Creek, Idaho or wherever, rather than seeing out a life sentence in a Kathmandu jail?

I can only speculate as to what perhaps took place. There is no evidence for such speculation in this memoir, but it seems to me the most plausible explanation.

The Taliban, Charles told me, in one of the calls he made from prison in Nepal, did turn up and Charles was in touch with them, but the Triads from Paris did not.

*

My speculation is informed by my previous contacts with Charles, Chantal and with the girl he called Roseanne. I pose here a lot of questions, but I am convinced they are certainties and the only way to explain the final drama in Kathmandu.

I met Roseanne three times in London and once in Paris. This was after Chantal had returned and not surprisingly I felt a distinct tension from her towards me, because she was probably aware that I had met Chantal, this woman who had returned after twenty-five years to claim Charles and take him from her.

There was certainly an unease and, if I have in my short and happy life any understanding of the way humans feel, it seemed to me that this Roseanne was strong and unlikely to put up with the situation. She wasn't Chantal or the women who had, by all accounts, succumbed to some mysterious charm of the killer.

I wonder therefore if this relationship, or the ending of it, might be related to the aborted deal in Kathmandu. It may be that Roseanne found a new partner when she found out that Charles was planning to find a new life in the United

States with Chantal. It may be that this new partner was associated with the Triads in Paris. Could she therefore be part of a possible betrayal and trap?

So, was Charles not in any hurry to leave Kathmandu because he and the Taliban were hanging around waiting for the Triads to arrive? We know that he stayed for weeks playing blackjack in the casinos. Presumably he was also in daily touch with the Parisians, asking why they hadn't arrived.

The most plausible explanation for why the Triads left Charles high and dry in Kathmandu was that through Roseanne they were made aware of the CIA double-cross about to be sprung on them. They didn't turn up, leaving Charles to explain to the Taliban that their scheme for an international outlet for heroin sales had been delayed.

The CIA contact was perhaps the only person, apart from Chantal, myself and his San Marino arms-dealer associates, who had been made aware that Sobhraj, with an assumed identity, was hanging around Kathmandu. Was it really a journalist who recognised him, or the policeman who had interviewed him 25 years previously, or did something or someone discover the plan and disrupt it, alerting the CIA that Charles's cover was blown. And did that result in the CIA instructing the Nepalese administration through the US government to arrest him for his past crimes and put him away for life?

*

In the wake of the 2021 broadcast of The Serpent, the BBC drama series about Sobhraj's crimes in Thailand, Andrew Anthony, a British and international journalist, republished his long article on Charles based on his interviews with him in Paris and then in Kathmandu. In the latest interview Charles protests that he was framed and shouldn't have been incarcerated in Kathmandu jails at all as there was no existing evidence that he had committed the murders of which he was convicted.

As part of the comprehensive piece, Anthony reproduced an interview he did with me in 2014.

In it I mention some of the substance of this memoir and, perhaps coincidentally, Anthony has the main points of my recollections substantiated by Sobhraj from his cell in Kathmandu.

Anthony diligently questions Boris Johnson, now Prime Minister of the UK, who does recall the episode of being presented with the story I've outlined above. Johnson tells Anthony that he knew, on hearing it, that the story was not for The Spectator. He doesn't add that he put Charles in touch with a Daily Telegraph writer.

Peter Oborne, whom Anthony also checked for verification, doesn't seem to remember the exact circumstances, but says it must have been an important story for Boris to have cycled to his place in the morning.

A trifle ridiculously, Sobhraj tells reporters who interview him in Kathmandu jail that on his impending release he will go to Kolkota and devote himself to work for the Mother Teresa mission. Repentant sinner or relentless self-publicist?

Anthony confesses at the end of the piece, written for the British magazine GQ and republished in 2021 by the Guardian-Observer newspaper group, that he can't quite make the connections between the allusions to red mercury, the CIA, the Taliban and to Boris Johnson etc. Anthony writes:

*"Towards the end, when he could perhaps sense my scepticism about the story he had told me, he insisted that*

*I speak to the writer and filmmaker Farrukh Dhondy. "He knows everything," he said. "You must talk to him."*

*We said our goodbyes and he told me to call him. I did, but there has been only silence."*

# 20

A year after Charles was sentenced to life imprisonment, he phoned me from Kathmandu jail. I was between Mumbai and London at the time, working in Mumbai as a script editor for my friend Bobby Bedi's film production company Kaleidoscope. The specific project I was dealing with was an adaptation of Macbeth to an Indian mafia setting entitled Maqbool, written by Abbas Tyrewalla and directed by Vishal Bhardwaj.

"Fa'ook it's Charles."

"Of course! You've got hold of a mobile phone?"

"Yes, take this number down. I want you to do something for me."

"As long as it's legal."

"Yes, ole man, just find out if there are any companies in India which make hot air balloons for even one passenger."

It was a ludicrous request. I laughed down the phone, but it didn't put Charles off.

"Just do that and call me. See what is available. Coming to Nepal across the Indian border is easy."

I said it was an absurd quest but I'd see what I could do.

What if I did find a suitable hot air balloon? I wondered if it really could be smuggled into a Kathmandu prison and used by Charles to escape into the skies and over the borders and whether Heath Robinson, the artist of machines for impossible tasks, was turning in his grave at such a ridiculous proposition. And the physicist in me also contemplated how long a hot air balloon takes to fill with the air that would carry it and Sobhraj aloft – surely hours.

I could picture the event: Charles uses the exercise courtyard to inflate the gaily coloured balloon using the burner that comes with these gizmos. He is accompanied by an accomplice or two, fellow prisoners he has done favours for, who will release the anchor of the balloon once it's inflated and Charles has climbed into its cradle.

The warders meanwhile are all asleep at their posts, at the gates, in the offices and corridors of the prison, having been fed soporific drugs or even poisons in the sweets Charles has ordered to celebrate his birthday or some other sacred occasion. None of them wakes up to witness Charles being carried into the sky and over the prison walls, with the wind and whatever control he has over the flight, carrying him across the border to mountainous territory in India, where he will get the balloon to land in the wilderness, unstrap himself from the safety belts and make his way to where some confederate would pick him up from the nearest village with a road.

Perhaps it wouldn't go that smoothly. One of the warders, on a diet to lose weight, would have pretended to eat the proffered sweets but surreptitiously thrown them in the bin. He would pretend to sleep but slyly observe Charles as the rest of his colleagues fall into deep sleep one by one. He would use the phone to alert the police outside the jail and as the balloon rises into the air and crosses the prison wall, squads of riflemen would be waiting to shoot it down.

The balloon would be riddled with bullet holes and, deflated, would immediately lose height and land ignominiously in the streets of Kathmandu as stray dogs gather to watch this wounded eagle land……….

I tell myself I mustn't get carried away. Suppose I did find him a hot air balloon and he did manage to get away in it. It would be a sensational story – the great escape! Would I then be criminally liable? Was there an extradition treaty between the UK and Nepal or even between India and Nepal? What would I be accused of? Helping a prisoner escape --- but that would be in Nepal. Buying a hot air balloon in India wouldn't be considered criminal. Even so, why should I risk it?

I was certain that my speculation was right. That Charles, whether he committed the murders in Nepal or not, had been, in all probability shopped by the CIA because he hadn't delivered what he intended or promised them. It was, I thought, extremely likely that the Nepalese authorities had been approached to put him away for life – he was no use to the CIA now that his cover had been blown.

Should I risk sending him a balloon?

Of course I wouldn't but curiosity about the possibility of the ridiculous drama got the better of me.

I asked one of the researchers, a young man called Sid who was working with me, to find out, through the internet or otherwise, whether there were any firms in India which manufactured and sold hot air balloons. He came up with several. I asked him to find the dimensions of the balloons. He did. The smallest one on offer was 30 metres by 20 metres and in addition there would be a perhaps small filing-cabinet-sized burner and the three-foot-tall cane cradle.

Charles was getting restless and phoned me several times to ask how far I'd got.

"Could it all come in two suitcases?" he enquired.

He'd given me the way out. I eventually had to tell him to forget the plan. There was no way that even the balloon itself without the burner and the cradle could fit into two suitcases. I didn't say that even if they would I wasn't going to help him escape. I think he understood. I didn't get another call about hot air balloons.

*

In 2008 my fictionalised account of a serial murderer called Johnson Thaat, *The Bikini Murders*, was published. All the reviewers identified the character as Sobhraj. As I've recorded above, I was interviewed on TV and both Sobhraj from his prison and his French lady lawyer were remotely brought onto screen to confront me. As the interview progressed and Charles expressed his spitting venom, I didn't feel in the least threatened, but felt certain that this was the end of our acquaintance. He couldn't sue me and I'd never see him again. Was that a relief?

It was therefore with some surprise that a few years later I received a call from him.

"Fa'ook, I read your book carefully and you have said there was no case for me to answer in any proper legal court case. Thank you."

"A book of fiction doesn't count for anything legally," I said. I was thinking that he had at the time denounced my novel and threatened to sue me, virtually calling me, on national TV, a pimp.

"Maybe, but see, my lawyers are appealing to the United Nations because this is a miscarriage of justice. If they look into it you could tell them some facts."

"I can only tell them what I know and remember."

"Exactly, exactly," he said. "Just keep this phone number and I will be in touch."

Some months later he called again to say that the United Nations had acknowledged the urgent persuasiveness of his case and he would soon be free. When I said I was surprised as I didn't know that any agency of the UN had such powers, he said he would send me the reply that the UN had sent his lawyers.

He e-mailed me a letter from some agency of the United Nations. It simply said words to the effect of "Thank you for your letter and submission. We acknowledge receipt of it." There was no more. For a brain as acute as the one which researched extradition laws of India and articles of the Thai penal code which imposed a statute of limitations on a sentence of murder, this seemed an impossible misreading.

If he had called back, I would have told him that acknowledging a letter was not acknowledging the justice of the complaint or a pledge to act upon it. It was a routine response to every communication.

He didn't call back and the United Nations haven't called me.

# Epilogue

Inevitably, anyone who hears, from me or any other source, that I was acquainted with Charles Sobhraj, asks me in varied wording, two questions. The first is "How did he manage to seduce so many women --- is he really charismatic and charming?" The words 'hypnotic' and 'compelling' also make an appearance in that first query.

The actor who played Charles in The Serpent was certainly handsome and charming and one can understand that his looks and manner would appeal to women. The real Charles never struck me as unusually charismatic or charming. He seemed quite ordinary, an average bloke you'd pass on the street without your attention being drawn to him – as one wouldn't on passing, say, James Dean or Elvis Presley (showing my age?) or possibly Johnny Depp.

Yet, on close contact, there was something in his gaze which was vaguely compelling. I wouldn't go so far as to call it hypnotic, but it certainly was a look in his eyes that would draw your attention.

Still, he was rumoured as having seduced very many women, especially after he was exposed and convicted as a murderer. I won't venture to propose any theory of why women fall for men on death row, murderers or serial killers, offering them sex or proposing marriage.

I have no pretension to amateur psychology. And yet in Chantal and in the other girlfriend of his, Roseanne, whom I met, I could see an absolute fascination leading to commitment. As I have said earlier on meeting Chantal, without the least facility or scientific basis for insights into behaviour, I can only ascribe it to the notion that somewhere, subconsciously if not consciously, they were attracted to the idea of a creature who could dispense death. But that may just be the pretentious speculation of someone who has read too many myths.

To the second question I am repeatedly asked, "didn't you feel a tinge of fear in his presence?" I have one answer. I didn't. Nevertheless, I never invited him home, not out of fear or even caution, but I wanted to keep our acquaintance at least one step away from 'friendship'. When we did sit in cafés or restaurants the thought did cross my mind that he had used such occasions to lace his victims' food or drink with soporifics or poisons, but obviously he wasn't going to try this on in a Chinese restaurant in Soho. No, I didn't ever think I was in any danger from Charles because I was never going to share a room with him or fall asleep in his presence.

The truth is that every time I encountered him, I was constantly aware that he had murdered scores of people. That thought was an enduring shadow in his presence, but it was a taint from his past as I was sure that he wouldn't risk the consequences of killing again. He wasn't a psycho in the sense that he had a blood-lust. He killed for gain, large or small, and never seemed to do it for any compulsion other than that. The life or death of his victims didn't matter and if that's crazy, yes! -- he was crazy, but he certainly seemed to be perfectly conscious of the risk involved in each of his murderous ventures. Calculation, if the descriptions he gave me or the ones I read in the books about him, rather than any passion, propelled his actions.

Less frequently and perfectly legitimately, I am asked why I went along and perhaps even played along with his seemingly outrageous schemes or demands. If I ask myself this, the answer is quite sincerely – curiosity. One doesn't encounter serial killers every day. Yes, there was always the professional potential of writing about him or extracting some confession or repentance for his past – not in any priestly enthusiasm – but to turn it into a film or a story. However shameful that may sound, it's the truth.

There were other incidents which, I hope understandably, stimulated curiosity by seeming intriguing or bizarre. What would he do with an introduction to the CIA? Why? Some were just ludicrous – his asking me for hot air balloons from his Kathmandu prison. Then there was the incident in which he asked for a connection to the Indian government to intervene to make a deal to save hostages held in the Indian Airlines plane in Kandahar. If he could save the lives of hundreds of hostages, why would I not put him in touch with any avenue of access to the Minister who was negotiating with the hostage-takers?

As for refusing to help him set up his money-laundering attempt and refusing to provide him with an antique-furniture-front for lethal arms dealing, I am acutely aware that I knew I had been asked to participate in international crime and declined. Could I have stopped international arms sales to terrorists? The anwer is 'no'. Shying away from ridicule is my only defence.

Sobhraj and his lawyers know that prose works written by Richard Neville or anyone else, even if they purport to be accounts of events related by Charles himself, can't be used as evidence in law. Sobhraj can always say this is pure invention by the writer. In the case of this account, I have the strong feeling that Charles wants the story of his introduction to the CIA and his possible intention to betray the processes and mechanisms of arms dealing by terrorist groups to the Agency, told by someone other than himself. He perhaps calculates that even now, it may act as a starting point of considerations towards his release.

I was there and have written it, I believe, as it was.

Why not sign up to our mailing list here:

More about Farrukh Dhondy and his books:

Why not browse our BOOKSHOP?

Find out more about Bite-Sized Books here:

Printed in Great Britain
by Amazon